"Adjusting to the personal and social demands o[f] and the young adult years is more complex than today's adolescents and young adults with bipola[r] are even greater and the stakes even higher. With their book *Facing Bipolar*, Federman and Thomson provide us with an important new resource. Based on sound clinical research and the rich experience of two knowledgeable practitioners, the book speaks in a direct and easy-to-understand voice that addresses the everyday questions of those initially facing this disruptive disorder. I strongly recommend this high-impact resource for teens, young adults, and others confronting the reality of bipolar disorder, and for the bookshelves of the counselors, psychologists, and psychiatrists who treat them."

—Alan M. Schwitzer, Ph.D., licensed clinical psychologist
and editor of the *Journal of College Counseling*

"Federman and Thomson have written a very thoughtful and pragmatic book. Their poignant stories describe the critical processes of recognition and acceptance while their straightforward advice conveys important treatment strategies required to manage this complex condition. This really is a must-read for young adults coming to terms with bipolar disorder."

—Richard Kadison, MD, chief of Harvard University Mental
Health Services and author of *College of the Overwhelmed*

"In my work with college students who occasionally get derailed, I have found that no issue is more perplexing for students and those who love them than the onset of bipolar disorder. Federman and Thomson provide a valuable frame of reference for making sense of the chaos that bipolar disorder can bring to the life of a college student. Students and family members will also find comfort and order in the sound words they provide."

—Penny Rue, Vice Chancellor of student affairs at the
University of California, San Diego

"Being a young adult with bipolar disorder is challenging, and it's imperative to seek out good resources to cope successfully. Having read numerous books about bipolar, I've not found any others that are as clear and informative as this one. Federman and Thomson have truly provided the information necessary to living a healthy and happy life with bipolar disorder."

—Chadrick Lane, recent college graduate with bipolar disorder, mental health research fellow, and MD candidate

FACING BIPOLAR

the **young adult's guide**
to dealing with bipolar disorder

Russ Federman, Ph.D.

J. Anderson Thomson, Jr., MD

New Harbinger Publications, Inc.

Publisher's Note

Care has been taken to confirm the accuracy of the information presented and to describe generally accepted practices. However, the authors, editors, and publisher are not responsible for errors or omissions or for any consequences from application of the information in this book and make no warranty, express or implied, with respect to the contents of the publication.

The authors, editors, and publisher have exerted every effort to ensure that any drug selection and dosage set forth in this text are in accordance with current recommendations and practice at the time of publication. However, in view of ongoing research, changes in government regulations, and the constant flow of information relating to drug therapy and drug reactions, the reader is urged to check the package insert for each drug for any change in indications and dosage and for added warnings and precautions. This is particularly important when the recommended agent is a new or infrequently employed drug.

Some drugs and medical devices presented in this publication may have Food and Drug Administration (FDA) clearance for limited use in restricted research settings. It is the responsibility of the health care provider to ascertain the FDA status of each drug or device planned for use in their clinical practice.

Distributed in Canada by Raincoast Books

Copyright © 2010 by Russ Federman and J. Anderson Thomson Jr.
New Harbinger Publications, Inc.
5674 Shattuck Avenue
Oakland, CA 94609
www.newharbinger.com

Cover design by Sara Christian; Text design by Amy Shoup and Michele Waters-Kermes; Acquired by Tesilya Hanauer; Edited by Kia Penso

---

Library of Congress Cataloging-in-Publication Data

Federman, Russ.
  Facing bipolar : the young adult's guide to dealing with bipolar disorder / Russ Federman and J. Anderson Thomson, Jr.
    p. cm.
  Includes bibliographical references.
  ISBN-13: 978-1-57224-642-3 (pbk. : alk. paper)
  ISBN-10: 1-57224-642-1 (pbk. : alk. paper) 1. Manic-depressive illness in adolescence--Popular works. I. Thomson, J. Anderson. II. Title.
  RJ506.D4F43 2010
  616.89'500835--dc22

                                                         2009044377

FSC
Mixed Sources
Product group from well-managed forests and other controlled sources
Cert no. SW-COC-002283
www.fsc.org
© 1996 Forest Stewardship Council

12   11   10

10   9   8   7   6   5   4   3   2

contents

acknowledgments

We are grateful that our collaborative work at the University of Virginia's Counseling and Psychological Services brought us together and inspired us to write this book. Our appreciation goes to Tesilya Hanauer and New Harbinger for taking a gamble on rookies to the self-help realm; New Harbinger's Jess Beebe and Kia Penso for their excellent copyediting, Drs. Steve Dauer and Tom Horvath for their support, encouragement, and editorial input; the artist Sabina Forbes II and her mother, Sabina Forbes, who brought their personal knowledge of the illness to bear on early chapters; our colleagues at the University of Virginia Counseling and Psychological Services, who provide unparalleled consultations; Drs. Goodwin and Jamison, whose collected body of research in their second edition text was essential to our writing; Stephen Stahl, whose incomparable textbook and educational tools guided our discussion of medications; the annual review course in neuroscience and psychopharmacology hosted by the Foundation for Advance Education and staffed by researchers at the National Institute of Mental Health; and Tracy Federman for making this book better than it would have been without her.

To our patients, who have honored us with their trust and granted us the privilege of being allowed into their lives in order to see and understand the realities of bipolar disorder, we dedicate this book.

introduction

So you've been told you're bipolar, or perhaps you're wondering if you are. You either have bipolar disorder or you think you do. You've learned that this diagnosis can mean a lifetime of troubles. You've learned that if you've got it, you might have to take medication for the rest of your life. You understand that the disorder is genetic. You understand that people with bipolar disorder sometimes need to be hospitalized. You didn't ask for this. It wasn't in your life plan.

Perhaps you've had times when you felt so down you couldn't get moving. Keeping up with your work or even getting out of the house seemed impossible. It felt like you were trying to slog your way through molasses with no end in sight. Essentially, your self-esteem was in the pits and you felt awful.

Then, there were other times when you felt alert and energized. Sleep didn't matter a whole lot and your usual challenges felt like a piece of cake. You felt alive! Images, scents, and sounds were so crisp and immediate. Others around you didn't seem to be moving at the same pace, but it didn't matter; little mattered. Yes, it was an exciting time and you enjoyed it. But just as quickly as it arrived, it was over, and you crashed back into the depression, back into the molasses.

You started thinking maybe you should end your life. You knew those thoughts weren't you, but at the same time they were you and they seemed the only solution. The confusion was hell. You can begin to see why people say bipolar is trouble. You know this craziness means something is wrong.

If you've sought help, you've probably received plenty of advice about how to manage this disorder. You've been told you should see a psychiatrist. And if you have, you're facing pills. Lots of pills. Take your choice: Lexapro, Seroquel, Depakote, lithium, Tegretol, Lamictal, and others. You've been told that while these drugs can be helpful, you'll also have side effects such as drowsiness, dry mouth, weight gain, dulling of your emotions, and even dulling of your sexuality. And you've been told that you may have to take several of them at the same time, forever. Why? If you feel fine or almost fine, why would you have to take these waist-expanding, thirst-inducing, libido-reducing pills forever? What is *that* all about?

They say something is wrong with your brain, your neurochemistry, your genetics. There's no simple explanation. Bipolar disorder is not a simple illness. It's a disorder of the brain and of the mind that affects who you are, what you think, what you feel, and how your personality places itself in the world. These are not things you can see, touch, taste, or smell.

They say you should get into psychotherapy. A psychotherapist is a different kind of shrink from the one who prescribes the pills; he or she is someone you'll talk with about how you're *really* feeling and thinking—the kind of stuff you just don't tell *anyone*. And you may have to do this for a while because you've also been told that bipolar isn't going to go away, no matter how much you want it to. Bipolar isn't like mononucleosis, which you'd recover from eventually.

And beyond the medicine and the psychotherapy, you're told that you'll have to monitor your sleep patterns carefully. You'll have to make sure that you get good sleep—that you go to sleep and get up at consistent times. You'll have to stop using alcohol, pot, stimulants, energy drinks, or whatever else you've relied upon to help you get by. To you it sounds like no partying, no fun, no life.

Besides, if you've only recently been told that you're bipolar, you probably think your parents, your loved ones, and the professionals you've seen are all exaggerating the bad news. It's like suddenly everyone is telling you that the sky is falling! And even if you decide to go along with their recommendations and do all that they're asking, you could still be psychiatrically hospitalized for acute depression, suicide attempts, or manic episodes. And in the middle of all this bad news, you're encouraged to remain hopeful and not let it get you down. Yeah, right!

Okay, let's get real. It's pretty unlikely that you'll simply do what other people expect without really questioning where they're coming from. You might hope that they're wrong and look for anything to support that hope. You may want a second opinion. You might also look toward any alternate explanations that will help you make sense of your recent instability. The bottom line is that a diagnosis of bipolar disorder sure as hell isn't welcome news. In fact, it's downright frightening, and you'll most likely do your best to find some way of minimizing it, explaining it away, or outright denying it.

Welcome to the resistance and denial that follow the news that you're bipolar. These reactions are absolutely normal, and so is your desire to run from the diagnosis. And as odd as this may sound, we advise against trying to sidestep your reactions. Intense reactions against the diagnosis are completely to be expected. Our focus will be to help you understand these reactions so that you can learn to deal with them effectively.

As you begin to face the reality of being bipolar, you'll find that one of the toughest challenges is saying good-bye to the person you once thought you would be, especially at a time in your life when you are thinking hopefully about your future. If you're new to the bipolar experience, you're probably somewhere between your midteens and your midtwenties, and letting go of your previous expectations about life's direction is hard. It may be even harder than it was to accept your bipolar diagnosis. Worse yet, you may even find that some people will withdraw from you or drop out of sight once you've found the courage to tell them, "I have bipolar disorder." Let's face it, some people are afraid of mental illness. Your relationships will be affected. Almost everything will be affected. We know this all must sound pretty grim; it doesn't need to be.

When you move to a new city, you need to know how to have the gas and electricity turned on and the phone hooked up. You need to find the grocery stores and the major department stores. A guidebook is essential, only now it's the *Lonely Planet Guide to Bipolar City* you need. You didn't choose this destination, but this is where you'll be living. You need to know how to live here. You need to know how to keep your mind stable, how to take care of it, and how to keep it on the right track. In your old world, where you wish you still lived, this isn't the book you would be flipping through in a bookstore. We understand. We know this is not a book you want to need.

In the chapters that follow, we'll provide you with straightforward, down-to-earth, and easily digestible information about this thing called bipolar disorder. You'll learn what it looks like, how common it is, how it usually unfolds, what's involved in treatment, what challenges you'll face, and what kinds of lifestyle changes you'll need to make. And if you're not the one with bipolar disorder, then this book will help you to better understand what's going on with the person you're concerned about.

Our intent is to make Bipolar City less frightening, less lonely, and less strange. You'll come to see that it's a different city from the one you were setting out for, but it's still quite livable. The hitch is that you don't get to live there unless you're able to let go of your expectations about the other place you had hoped to reach. And once you come to terms with this loss, once you're able to look around and realistically assess what it takes to make a home in your new destination, then you'll be in a much better position to tackle the reality of bipolar disorder. We hope to help you manage this important transition.

So why did we write this book? Because we have both worked in the mental health field since the mid-1970s. Between us, we have more than thirty-five years of experience working with university students. We've each treated many students with bipolar disorder, and we've come to see firsthand the profound impact that the disorder can have upon the development of adolescents and young adults. We absolutely understand that bipolar disorder doesn't represent an easy life story.

From our experience in the trenches of university mental health, often working together on the same cases, we've tried to bring to these pages our knowledge, extensive experience, and strong compassion for people like you, who are beginning to come to terms with bipolar disorder. We want to speak with you as if you are sitting with us. We want to reach through these pages and make a difference in your life.

CHAPTER ONE

what is bipolar disorder and how can you tell if you have it?

Bipolar disorder is a mood disorder. So what *is* mood? Mood is like the color in a painting or the tone and intensity of a piece of music. It reflects our emotions and thoughts, whether we feel anxious or relaxed, happy or sad, or anything in between. Mood isn't a reflection of any one thing; it's a combination of many. Just think of all the parts of your experience that lead to the expression "I'm in such a good mood" or, conversely, "I'm feeling really down."

So what's normal mood? Usually, throughout your day you have a variety of experiences that cause subtle—or even not-so-subtle—shifts in your mood. That's quite normal. Life without mood changes would be flat. It's the variability of your mood that gives your life texture and dimension. When your mood changes, it's usually because of how you feel about something that's happening in the world. Normal mood states don't change significantly without a clear cause-and-effect explanation. When good stuff happens, you generally feel good. Similarly, a day of frustration and disappointment can bring you down.

Just as the type of mood you experience varies, so does the intensity of your mood. Let's say you're in school and you're generally doing well but you fail a quiz. This is going to feel very different than if you just learned you failed out of school. The first situation will feel bad, while the second will probably feel awful—and for much longer. Again, strong mood changes usually make sense when they have a connection with what's happening in your life. When they don't and you keep having them, then things begin to feel screwy.

And sometimes things feel screwy if you have bipolar disorder. In fact, with bipolar, mood states can become way out of balance, because mood changes can occur independently of what's going on in life. If you're bipolar, you may also have thoughts and feelings that get more and more intense until you feel out of control. And what's worse, this increasing intensity can seem to come out of nowhere. Nothing caused it, that you can see, but like it or not you find that you're no longer in the driver's seat. Those intense shifts in mood, for no reason, are the roller-coaster reality of bipolar disorder. This isn't normal mood, and yes, it can be downright frightening.

You may also be frightened because of where you are in your life. For those who don't develop bipolar disorder when they're kids, the first explicit symptoms often appear between late adolescence (approximately sixteen or seventeen) through the mid-twenties. If you're in that age range, particularly at the younger end, then life isn't all that stable or well established. In fact, you may be in the midst of many changes all at the same time, such as dealing with the craziness of high school, preparing for college, living away from home for the first time, starting your first job, or heading off to graduate school or beyond. With all the big changes you're facing at this stage of your life, the last thing you need is the additional complexity of a major mental disorder. Add the bipolar dimension to the mix, and you've got quite a handful.

So back to the question you're looking at: Are you really bipolar? You're not going to be able to answer this one easily on your own. Diagnosing bipolar disorder requires the assistance of a mental health professional. However, you can at least get started by finding out enough good, clear information about the disorder so as to get a general sense of whether or not you fit the profile. You'll want to understand this illness as best you can, because understanding it is an important first step in getting you back in the driver's seat.

One additional comment before we move into a discussion of bipolar symptoms: If you're bipolar or think you may be, the material we're about to cover won't be easy to read and could be frightening as well. We want to assure you up front that bipolar disorder is not a sentence to lifelong misery. You can expect good treatment from many professionals who are continually getting a better understanding of the disorder. In the second half of this book, we'll be talking about the many different things you yourself can do in order to live well. So our message is to hang in there. It's realistic to hope for a good life with bipolar disorder. We trust you'll get there once you've taken in the full picture.

depression and mania: the two poles of bipolar disorder

You may have heard the term "manic depression." Manic depression is an old name for bipolar disorder that conveyed the notion of two opposing polarities of mood: depression and mania.

In recent years mania has been split into two distinct subtypes: hypomania and mania. *Hypo* means "below," like a hypodermic needle that goes below the skin. Similarly, *hypomania* refers to manic symptoms that are below the intensity of full mania, or what we refer to as a manic episode.

We'll get to a more detailed explanation of hypomania and mania a little later. For now, you should know that within bipolar disorder we see three distinct elements: major depression, hypomania, and mania. There's also something less common, known as a mixed episode, which we'll discuss this toward the end of this chapter. For now, it's important to keep in mind that these all exist on a continuum, sort of like the left and right balance controls on a pair of speakers. Or you can think of a thermometer, measuring different degrees of temperature. One end of the temperature gauge is cold and the other is quite hot. Bipolar disorder's range of moods is similar, except that we don't have a simple gauge that measures mood intensity.

Depression

Depression is the part of the bipolar spectrum that most people can identify with, whether or not they are bipolar. All of us probably recall a time when things simply weren't going well and as a result we felt unhappy and blue or had other down feelings. In some respects, feeling unhappy for a while from time to time is a very basic part of our human experience.

So what's the difference between sadness that results from some situation in life and what we might instead call clinical depression? To begin with, the experience of depression is something that's much more global or all-encompassing. It's like a thick gray cloud has settled on you and most of what's under the cloud is dull or muted. The emotional landscape of your world becomes flattened. The thick cloud can affect just about everything.

We've already told you that depression is fairly common, but the specific form of depression central to the bipolar diagnosis is what we refer to as *major depression*. Just as you'd guess from its name, major depression is the real deal and can be quite serious; but depression as part of the bipolar spectrum can be even more so. In fact, based on a review of 28 studies from 1945 to 2000, the suicide rate of bipolar patients was approximately twenty-two out of every one hundred patients (Goodwin and Jamison 2007). Keep in mind, though, that this review covered studies that go back more than half a century, when bipolar disorder was not as effectively treated as it is now. The good news is that suicide of bipolar individuals is decreasing because more effective medications are available, and because medical professionals have a better understanding of the disorder.

Major depression has several sets of symptoms, and we'll be discussing these below. You don't have to have all the symptoms to be diagnosed with major depression; however, if at some point you've experienced half of the symptoms at the same time within a two-week period, then it's likely that you've experienced a major depressive episode.

Feeling Unmotivated

When you're depressed, you feel tired and unmotivated. The energy you need to move toward the world with gusto just isn't there. Rather than going to school, doing homework, going to work, or whatever, you find that you're too tired to bother. Instead you turn off and disengage from it all. It's not at all like going on vacation and kicking back. It's more like you simply feel too tired to move forward toward the daily tasks of life.

Not Enjoying Things

This cloud that has settled over you also has the effect of sapping the pleasure out of your life. Things that normally feel enjoyable no longer create any sparks, and the things you typically looked forward to don't seem to matter anymore. It's like the pleasurable aspects of your day-to-day experience have been wiped out, even with your favorite activities.

Feeling Run-Down

You may also find that when you're depressed, you're low on energy. Even with a decent night's sleep, reasonable nutrition, and exercise, you can still feel that your usual energy is reduced by half or more. As a consequence, just getting through the day turns into a challenge. If you're acutely depressed, you might find that you actually move more slowly, like you're in slow motion while the rest of the world is moving at normal speed.

Agitation and Irritability

Less frequently, the opposite of sapped energy can also occur. You just feel agitated and irritable. Everything seems to bug you. Imagine feeling that everything is messed up while at the same time your own negative outlook has you convinced that things will only keep getting worse. You already feel down, and this additional negativity can color everything and cause you to feel worried, irritable, shaken up, and unable to relax. It's like you're a washing machine stuck on a perpetual agitation cycle.

Having Trouble Thinking and Remembering

The low energy or agitation described above can also affect your mental processes. If you're experiencing acute depression, then your thinking becomes slowed or dulled. If you're stuck in the agitation cycle, then your thoughts are all jumbled and tossed about. Mental tasks that are usually simple for you can become very difficult, while complex thought processes may feel overwhelming.

Depression can affect your memory. Imagine being asked the driving directions to your house, where you've lived for nine years, only to find that you can't clearly think of the sequence of turns and street names that are usually so familiar to you. Depression may also interfere with your attention and concentration as well as your memory. It's hard to be sharp when you feel dull. It's also hard to have mental clarity when agitation interferes with your ability to think and remember.

Feeling Bad About Yourself and Avoiding Friends and Family

When most things no longer feel pleasurable, and when your cognitive capacity is noticeably impaired, it's likely you're not going to feel good about yourself. When you are experiencing low self-esteem, you usually don't want to be around others, and it's hard to imagine that others want to be around you.

Feeling Guilty or Worthless

When you're depressed, it's not just that you believe things are going poorly for you; it's more that you believe things are going poorly and it's your fault. Of course, it's not true that you are to blame, but guilt is a common feature of depressed thinking.

Thinking About Ending It All

When the pain of depression becomes really bad, ending your life can start to seem like one way to stop the misery. Suicidal thinking is a common aspect of depression. It isn't evidence that you've become crazy. It's more like faulty problem solving. Killing yourself can seem like a viable solution when you've come to think that all other solutions are doomed to failure. The problem with this thinking is that the solution is a permanent one, but your depression is temporary! Any of the depressive symptoms can be cause for seeking professional help, but suicidal thinking is one of the most serious. Suicidal thinking is a strong message that you should seek help. Feeling suicidal is not something that you want to try to manage on your own. There's too much at stake.

Out-of-Whack Body Rhythms

Lastly, with depression, all of your natural biological rhythms can become screwed up. Appetite, sexuality, and sleep cycles can all be affected. You may find that you've lost your appetite, or that it increases because you're using food to soothe yourself. So you may lose or gain weight without wanting to. Sexual desire typically is also down during depression, and sleep can go either way. You may find that you're sleeping too much, like you just can't get enough, because sleep becomes a convenient escape from the world, which feels so painful. On the other hand, the very fact that you feel troubled can interfere with your ability to fall asleep or sleep for long enough.

Are you depressed? Have you ever been depressed? To help you with some of your own self-assessment, we've provided a checklist that includes most of the key symptoms of major depression. Take a look at the list and check any of the symptoms that you have now or have had in the past.

depression checklist

- ☐ feeling down, blue, sad, unhappy, and so on
- ☐ fatigue and low motivation
- ☐ loss of pleasure (everything feeling flat)
- ☐ low energy or agitated energy
- ☐ poor concentration and attention
- ☐ low self-esteem and withdrawal from others
- ☐ guilt and feelings of worthlessness
- ☐ suicidal thoughts
- ☐ change in appetite (up or down) with weight loss or weight gain
- ☐ not enough or excessive sleep

If you find that you've experienced six or more of these different depressive symptoms at the same time, and if this cluster of symptoms lasted for two weeks or longer, then it's quite possible that you've experienced a major depressive episode. If so, it doesn't necessarily mean you're bipolar. In fact, many people have episodes of depression and never experience hypomania or mania. We call this *unipolar depression*, and it's far more common than bipolar disorder. While people with unipolar depression struggle mostly with feelings on one side of the mood scale, most people with bipolar disorder have difficulties with both sides: they've had at least one major depressive episode and one or more hypomanic or manic episodes

Depression is a big part of the bipolar experience. Most people with bipolar spend far more time in depression than they do in hypomania or mania. And because of the suicide potential with major depression, it's also one of the more dangerous parts of the disorder. If you checked more than just a few of the items in the checklist, we strongly advise you to see a mental health professional, at least for an initial consultation.

Mania

So what's wrong with feeling up? Why wouldn't you want to be happy, optimistic, and energetic? Well, if you could get there and sustain your up mood at a level that was manageable, then yes, there'd probably be nothing wrong with that. In fact, isn't that what most of us strive for?

The problem is that if you're bipolar, then the delicious experience of being up can be a mixed bag—pleasurable but also potentially dangerous. The progression toward mania may start with manageable pleasure; however, there's not much distance to travel on the mood scale before the happiness, increased energy, and expansive feelings of being up turn into more intensity than you can handle. Hypomania can be the deceptive warm-up to a full manic episode. The following three personal accounts will give you a feel for hypomanic mood elevation.

➔ Mary Beth

I started to notice it when I was about sixteen. I would kind of be going along with my life and I'd have these periods where, out of nowhere, this wonderful energy would lift me up and I would feel giddy and excited. I didn't know why I felt so high. I just knew it felt great. My energy was way up and the normal things that were usually a drag to do—like homework or helping my mom around the house—just seemed easy. And when I would get through with my work stuff, there would be tons of things to do next—things to look up online, short stories to write, rearranging everything on my iPod—maybe even doubling or tripling the amount of music I had saved, and shopping. Oh yeah, shopping! Everything I thought of doing seemed like incredible ideas and it was such a relief to be able to get by with only three or four hours' sleep. Then I had the extra time to actually follow through on some of the things I was thinking about. It was a rush to hang out with my friends; there were endless things to talk about…and man could I talk. Sometimes I'd get on a roll and couldn't stop. Thoughts were flying into my head and my words were flying out almost as fast. At times it felt a bit scary, like I was stuck in fast-forward. But on the other hand I really loved the energy. Instead of feeling stuck in the boring routines of my life, I felt like I could do just about anything. In fact, when I think of the really smart kids at school who are involved in everything and seem to have it all together, I imagine this is what they must feel like.

→ Jacqueline

I guess I've always been kind of moody, but I never thought I was sick. I just figured my ups and downs were a part of me—like a reflection of my personality. Being up was also no problem when I was in college because staying awake until four or five in the morning wasn't all that different from my usual sleep time, which was about two. But in the three or four years since I've been out of school and working as a paralegal, I find that the periods of being up are more intense. The problem is that now, getting a couple of hours' sleep doesn't work when I have long workdays that require sharp attention to detail. It's also kind of strange that during the periods when I'm up, I do things that I'd never do when I'm just being my normal self. This is kind of embarrassing, but I find that when I'm up, so is my sexual energy. I'm no prude, but it's just an entirely different experience. By about eleven or midnight, instead of winding down and going to bed, I find I want to go out to the bars because I've got all this energy and sleeping is the last thing on my mind. I also feel really horny…like my sexuality's been turned on and I can't find the volume knob to lower its intensity. Usually I will get to know a guy before I have sex with him. Not when I'm up. In fact when I'm up, I just want what I want and I go for it. The scary part is that I often forget to use protection. It's the same with stuff I want to buy. Sex and credit card spending…boy, do I have a field day. I guess the good news is that my periods of being up rarely last longer than three or four days. So while I almost always have regrets about my impulsive choices, I'm usually able to regroup and get back to my more normal self before I do too much damage. I don't know whether or not something's wrong with me. But I do know that this pattern won't work for me if I'm going to try to settle down with someone and raise a family.

→ Richard

I don't think anyone would say being a second-year med student is a fun thing to do. The amount of work is overwhelming. Most of the time it consumes your life. I remember in college I was involved in a lot of other activities, but not these days. I go to class. I go to the library and study. I hang out with friends, usually in study groups. Typically a few of us will have dinner together, and then I'm home again, studying until bedtime. Granted, I find occasional breaks, but not often.

During the last few months of my first year in med school I noticed that I would have these periods where, out of nowhere, all the work became easy, and this wasn't because my professors were letting up. The experience wouldn't last long—maybe a few days. But when those periods would occur, I felt like my mind was flying. I could absorb the material easily, working into the early morning hours. Frankly, it was like I had taken amphetamines without any of the negative side effects. This past summer, when I was doing some research at a cardiology lab on the West Coast, I found that I slipped into a pretty strong depression. I don't know why, but I really felt awful, and I mean like thinking-about-killing-myself awful. Just like the highs, it kind of came out of nowhere. Maybe it had to do with the fact that I was away from home without much social support. But you know, maybe it was just neurochemical… I don't know. I do know that both my mother and my maternal grandfather were diagnosed with depression. So clearly I'm at risk, genetically. Fortunately, I started to come out of the depression just about the time that I was ready to seek some help. I was really relieved to have myself back.

But recently, over the past couple of months since being back in school, I've again had some of those brief periods where I feel like everything is turned up at high speed. This past week it happened again, though I'm kind of back to myself now. Like I said, everything felt accelerated. The scary part is that I started thinking I could do things that in retrospect were really unrealistic.

For instance, since my summer cardiology research I've been fascinated by developments in new artificial heart designs. So I came up with my own that I thought was really innovative. I even developed a plan as to how I was going to fund the product research. I got so excited by these possibilities that I shared them with a friend of mine who's a cardiac resident. He looked at me like I was nuts. What's worse is that I couldn't comprehend why he didn't see the brilliance of my design.

Well, in retrospect, it probably wasn't all that brilliant…maybe not even realistic. I know I'm smart, but I also know that I'm not about to invent the next artificial heart! Even more frightening, I know just enough about psychiatric disorders to begin to wonder if my family history combined with my own mood fluctuations may mean that I'm bipolar. I don't like it, but maybe it's true.

Hypomania: The Common Denominator

The reason we identify hypomania as the common denominator is that almost everybody who has bipolar disorder experiences it. Even full mania, which we will talk about shortly, usually doesn't occur suddenly; instead, there is a gradual escalation of elevated mood progressing toward a full manic episode. This initial mild to moderate aspect of elevated mood is hypomania.

As you saw in the stories of Mary Beth, Jacqueline, and Richard, hypomania can take many forms. But one thing is common for most people once hypomania starts: at first it feels good. Who wouldn't want to feel energetic, mildly euphoric, gregarious, creative, and confident, with rapid thought processing and diminished need for sleep? You got it. Hypomania can be very seductive. It can draw you in before you realize that anything is wrong, because many things feel just right or even better. And besides, the people around you will also probably think you're doing fabulously, at least until your hypomania starts going over the top.

One exception that we can add about this positive feel in the early stages of hypomania is irritability. Being irritable isn't pleasurable. You don't feel open or warm toward others. You generally feel just the opposite. Sometimes sustained irritability combined with elevated energy can be a unique form of hypomania that's the lead-up to a more acute manic episode.

Just as we did in the section on major depression, we're providing a list of the different symptoms often present in hypomania. We've skipped a detailed discussion of each symptom, as most are illustrated in the stories of Mary Beth, Jacqueline, and Richard. Again, take a look at the list and check any of the symptoms that you have now or have had in the past.

hypomania checklist

☐ a distinct period of up, happy, optimistic, or irritable mood lasting at least four days

☐ inflated self-esteem; feelings of grandiosity

☐ decreased need for sleep; feeling rested after only a few hours

☐ feeling more talkative than usual; feeling pressured to keep talking

☐ racing thoughts or thoughts that seem to take flight

☐ easily being distracted by seemingly irrelevant or unimportant things

☐ increased goal-directed activity (cleaning, organizing, working on projects)—more than is usual for you

☐ excessive involvement in pleasurable activities that have a high potential for negative outcomes, like unrestrained shopping sprees, sexual hookups, or foolish business investments

Compared to the major depression checklist, the criteria for a hypomanic episode are a bit more complicated. First, the experience should represent a significant change in your functioning from what is normal for you, and any accompanying changes in behavior should be easily identifiable by others. In other words, it's not just a mild shift; you feel it and others notice it. On the other hand, the changes should not be severe enough to cause significant impairment in your functioning or require hospitalization. If they do, then you've probably crossed over into full mania, which we'll discuss in more detail in the section to come. And finally, the first item on the list, which identifies at least four days of distinctly changed mood, must be true for you as well as three additional items on the list. If the changes in mood haven't lasted for at least four days, you don't fit the hypomanic profile, even if you checked off most of the other items on the list. It seems that we're all allowed brief periods of intense mood change before we're diagnosable! But if you do meet the above criteria—four days of distinctly different mood plus three additional selections—then it's quite possible that you may have experienced a hypomanic episode.

Mania: The Unmistakable Symptoms

If you've ever had a full manic episode or have been around somebody who was in the midst of one, its presence is unmistakable. Think of the symptoms of hypomania that we just presented in the previous section. Now imagine those same behaviors being increased twofold, threefold, or more, and you begin to get the picture.

The person experiencing a manic episode is not having fun or feeling relatively euphoric or expansive. He or she is not just experiencing mild or moderately accelerated thought and accompanying rapid speech. It's more like the valve that controls the flow of energy, mood, and thought has been set to wide-open, and any semblance of normalcy or appropriateness has been eliminated by the intensity of mania. The intensity of mania is not compatible with effective functioning, and the manic individual feels very much out of control.

Sleep Matters

When energy is up, the need for sleep is down. These two elements, elevated energy and reduced sleep, are present in almost all occurrences of hypomania and mania. In hypomania, the reduced sleep may not be extreme or it may not go on long enough to create significant impairment. But if you experience sleep deprivation for extended periods of time, you can't think normally.

The mind and body absolutely need time to recharge. Without it, the functioning of the mind in particular begins to unravel. Just think of how you feel after several days of much reduced sleep or a couple of consecutive all-nighters. Now imagine the same experience combined with intense energy and greatly accelerated thinking. Under the pressure of mania, sense can easily deteriorate toward nonsense.

This kind of unraveling happens when the connection of one thought to the next loses its cohesion and becomes part of a jumbled sequence of thoughts rushing forward like a cascading waterfall. While your thought process is tumbled and tossed about, any meaningful connection to reality can become weaker and weaker—if not broken altogether. To most people interacting with you, the moderate form of this manic thinking will look like confusion, while the extreme form will come across as nonsensical gibberish. Your capacity to see yourself accurately goes out the window. You're just caught up in whatever is going on. Consequently, you're no longer able to think about your choices and exercise good judgment. Here's where mania becomes dangerous.

When your ability to use good judgment and restraint is no longer intact, then we see heightened *impulsivity*. If you've ever been a little under the influence, you know what we're talking about; if not, you can refer to Mary Beth's story. Jacqueline describes an even stronger version. However, even though both Mary Beth and Jacqueline still had at least some control of their behavior, it's easy to predict that when you're manic, sleep deprived, and consequently not capable of good judgment, your world is going to get chaotic.

Psychosis

On the extreme end of the bipolar continuum, the deterioration of mental functioning progresses into psychosis. Thoughts are not only rapid and disorganized, but they represent significant distortion of reality. This distortion may take the form of delusional thinking and paranoid ideas, such as believing that you're being followed or that your friends are part of a plot to overthrow the government.

Psychosis includes hallucinations or the perception of something that isn't real. You've probably heard of people hearing voices or, when they're under the influence of hallucinogenic drugs, seeing things that aren't really there. These voices and visions are hallucinations, extreme distortions of reality. But with manic psychosis, this extreme distortion is not caused by drugs!

When mania progresses so far that it affects the core of mental functioning in these ways, it looks like what we think of as "craziness." If you think you may be bipolar or if you already know you are, you should know that this degree of mental unraveling is rare. The progression of mania is so obvious to people around the manic person that someone almost always steps in to get the manic person to treatment before acute deterioration occurs. This gives you some idea of how important it is to have a strong support network, which we'll discuss in chapter 5.

By now, you probably have a pretty clear sense of what mania looks like and how it's different from its smaller cousin, hypomania. We can skip the checklist for mania because most of the symptoms are the same as those in the hypomania checklist. The biggest difference is in intensity. In mania the mood disturbance is so severe that it causes marked impairment in most realms of functioning.

Mixed Episodes

In addition to the three distinct elements of bipolar disorder (depression, hypomania, and mania), there's also an odd expression of the illness that we refer to as a *mixed episode*: a blend of manic and depressive symptoms.

The most common form of a mixed episode occurs when a person experiences what we refer to as *rapid cycling*, a rapid shift back and forth between manic and depressive symptoms. These shifts can even occur several times within an hour, or they can be spread out over the course of an entire day. If you've experienced a mixed episode, you know it's quite the roller-coaster ride, with sharp ups and downs compressed into relatively brief time periods. A less common occurrence is when the manic and depressive symptoms are truly mixed. An example would be someone who's experiencing depressed mood, diminished appetite, and suicidal ideas (the depressed symptoms) while also experiencing elevated energy, racing thoughts, rapid or pressured speech, and decreased need for sleep (the manic symptoms).

Bipolar I and Bipolar II

So far, we've discussed the range of different symptoms and the different mood states found on the bipolar continuum. There's one more important distinction to make: it's the difference between bipolar I disorder and bipolar II disorder.

Bipolar I disorder corresponds with what used to be called manic depression: it's when a person has experienced a major depressive episode and a full manic episode in no particular sequence. With bipolar II, a person has had a major depressive episode and a hypomanic episode, but *has not* progressed further into a full manic episode.

Bipolar II tends to be viewed as a mild or more functional form of the disorder. However, it's also important to note that sometimes bipolar II can be a precursor of bipolar I. In other words, a major depressive episode that occurs before or after hypomanic symptoms can represent an early phase of bipolar I.

Just as a volcanic eruption can be heralded by the less explosive venting of a volcano, bipolar II can be a sign that bipolar I is about to develop. There is no way of knowing whether someone diagnosed with bipolar II will ever develop full manic symptoms and thus cross over into bipolar I, just as there is no way of knowing whether a volcano's venting of smoke and ash means it's about to erupt. But what we do know is that the sooner hypomanic symptoms can be stabilized and the longer a person's mood can be kept stable, the less likely it is that symptoms of full mania will suddenly emerge at some point in the future. If the volcano quiets down or only vents with mild to moderate force, then we have more hope that we won't see a full eruption.

You now have an overview of most of the symptoms related to the diagnosis of bipolar disorder. If you're not absolutely clear as to whether or not you fit the criteria for the disorder, that's fully understandable. If you had 100 people in a room, all diagnosed with bipolar disorder, you'd find each person's experience would be different from everyone else's. There would be some recurrent themes, but still, expressions of mood, range of emotions, and the frequency and intensity of mood changes would be different for each person.

The important thing to keep in mind is that our checklists and discussion of the different aspects of the disorder are not in any way meant to replace a full diagnostic assessment. If anything, they are meant to give you a clear enough idea of the symptoms and patterns involved in the disorder that you can determine whether additional consultation is needed. Bipolar disorder can be quite serious—serious enough to land you in a hospital and even affect much of your future. It's not something to ignore or minimize. It's certainly not something to run from, though we understand that that might be exactly what you want to do. If you're simply unsure about yourself or someone else, it's important to seek professional help.

having bipolar disorder vs. being bipolar

You are much more than your bipolar disorder. You do not need to let it define you. You can attain success, happiness, fulfillment, and achievement in life despite having bipolar disorder. But at the same time, the bipolar experience is one that often sits at your core—in your brain, in your emotions, and consequently very much in your sense of who you are. It's not in an elbow or a foot. Generally speaking, the experience of the disorder feels more like "being," as opposed to "having," yet you will hear people in normal conversation speak of both being bipolar and of having bipolar disorder.

When you've sprained an ankle, it typically doesn't feel central to your sense of self. It's something you have, not something you are. But think of times you've been sad or depressed. In those moments, you say, "I am sad," as opposed to "I have sadness." In other words, feeling *is* being. So the reality is that many people with bipolar disorder often think of themselves as "being bipolar," because that's how they feel it. When we use that common expression in this book, it's because we want to reflect that feeling, which is a part of their experience.

It's important for you to know that you, not the disorder, define and create your future. This awareness is important to hold on to; otherwise you might feel that life with bipolar disorder is like river rafting without any oars, where you're simply being carried along and tossed about by the river's currents, eddies, and occasional rapids. While the expression "being bipolar" does mean that you have an ongoing mental disorder, it is not meant in any way to minimize or detract from your sense of individuality or power, or the possibilities for your life.

CHAPTER TWO

getting help

So you've had some symptoms of depression or maybe even hypomania. Even though the hypomania felt good, you still sense that you're not quite okay. Perhaps other people have said as much to you. You wonder about seeing a mental health professional, but what do you do? Where do you go? How do you find the right person? What do you say? What will they ask you? What about medication? In this chapter we'll walk you through your first visit with a mental health professional, and we'll also give you an overview of the different medications currently being used to treat bipolar disorder. For most people, meeting with a mental health clinician is helpful and brings relief.

hesitation is normal

As much as you'll be encouraged to get help, it's not uncommon to feel reluctant to actually do it. Your hesitation and uncertainty about seeking help for bipolar disorder are a normal reaction. Just the thought of getting help can feel frightening. Actually making an appointment can make your concerns seem all too real.

If you can't face the visit alone, then consider bringing someone with you to your first appointment, anyone who would make the visit feel safer and more comfortable. That person can be your advocate: someone who will lend support, ask their own questions, recall what was discussed, and process the session with you—kind of like having someone fielding behind you to catch any balls that you miss.

where to turn for help

There are several kinds of practitioners within the mental health field. Although they have different degrees, most have had the necessary training to recognize bipolar symptoms, help you become more secure in the diagnosis, and help you find proper treatment. These disciplines include licensed professional counselors (LPC), licensed clinical social workers (LCSW), clinical psychologists (Ph.D. or Psy.D), and psychiatrists (MD). Many primary care physicians, pediatricians, gynecologists, and family physicians will also have some knowledge of the illness and be able to assist you.

Many clergy have training in pastoral counseling, which includes some familiarity with major psychiatric illnesses, including bipolar disorder. They too may be able to recognize what you are up against, but you will still want to seek a referral to a mental health professional who is qualified to diagnose and treat bipolar patients.

your first appointment

Each mental health professional has his or her own style. Ideally, you'll hit it off right away with the one you've chosen. But you may not. Though trust and comfort often develop over time, your initial experience with a mental health professional should be a reassuring one. You should be able to feel that the person can understand you, and that a trusting and helpful relationship is possible between you. If you don't start to feel this within a couple of visits, then that person may not be the best fit. We strongly suggest that you discuss any discomfort with the professional you're seeing; if you find that this doesn't help, it's clearly time to look for someone else.

Common Questions During a First Appointment

The first appointment should last somewhere between forty-five and ninety minutes. The first questions will probably be about the concerns that led you to make an appointment. The professional will ask you about your most immediate symptoms and the details of whatever depressive, hypomanic, or manic symptoms you may be having. Subsequent questions will cover a wide range of different issues and will help the professional arrive at an initial diagnosis and treatment recommendations.

In order to help you prepare, we've provided a list of the kinds of things you will be asked about during your first appointment. Of course, each professional will approach these in his or her own unique way. It will be helpful if you review the following questions and even write down your answers to the questions before your appointment.

questions for you to answer

- What brings you in today?

- How long have you been experiencing your difficulties? When did they start?

- Is there anything that you think has triggered or caused your difficulties?

- What are the specific problems you've been having? (Think about the different symptoms described in chapter 1.)

- Have you ever experienced similar difficulties before? When?

- Have you ever received any previous mental health treatment? When, with whom, and what did it involve?

- Do you have any other current mental health issues besides those that bring you in today? What are they, and are you currently receiving treatment? Do you think they may be related to your current difficulties?

- Does anyone in your family have a history of mental illness? Who are they, and what do you know about their treatment?

- Is there anyone in your family who you think may have difficulties due to mental health issues but who has not received treatment? What's the nature of their difficulties?

- What seems noteworthy about your own personal history? Has most of your life been good, complex, traumatic? What has your relationship been like with parents, siblings, and other significant people?

- What's been your experience in school, academically and socially?

- How are you doing with your sexuality? Any current or past concerns?

- What's been your experience with substance use (current and past)? Is there anyone in your family with a history of substance abuse?

- Any significant medical issues (current and past)?

Topics That Are Difficult to Talk About

At some point during your appointment you'll also be asked about symptoms that aren't so common. Do you ever hear voices? Do those voices comment on your actions or make disparaging remarks? Do you see things that are not there? We realize some of these are scary things to think about— and even scarier things to have happen to you. It's important for you to know that during acute depression or mania, hallucinations and strange thoughts can occur. If these kinds of symptoms have ever happened to you, it's imperative that your mental health professional know about them.

If the topic hasn't already come up, you'll be asked if you have thoughts of suicide. Have you ever made plans to kill yourself, or do you have concrete plans now? Sometimes this line of questioning can be jarring, especially if you're not necessarily describing symptoms of depression. Suicidal thoughts can go along with many different disorders, and most mental health professionals will ask about these thoughts. We strongly encourage you to be open and honest in your answers to these questions. Suicidal thinking doesn't mean you're crazy, nor does it mean you'll be hospitalized, unless it seems like you're actually going to act on your impulses. Suicidal thinking usually means that you're hurting a lot, feeling trapped, and beginning to think there is no way out of this misery; therefore, these thoughts require close attention.

Any good mental health professional will also ask you if you've ever had violent feelings toward others. Have you ever felt like hurting or killing anyone? Have you ever seriously injured someone? Do you own weapons? Needless to say, those are unpleasant questions, but if you are bipolar, you may have periods of intense irritability and aggression. You want to know, and you want the professionals treating you to know, whether your illness puts you at risk for such dangerous behaviors. It's important that you and the professional you're seeing make a plan to ensure that you won't harm anyone or create a nightmare of legal problems for yourself. Being in jail isn't a hurdle you want to put in your path toward the treatment you need.

diagnosis

When all is said and done, ideally the mental health professional will have reached a diagnosis, sorted out that diagnosis from other possibilities, and shared his or her thinking with you. Your professional may also tell you that he or she is uncertain and needs more time with you before saying anything for sure. This uncertainty isn't bad news. If anything, it's a sign of someone who is careful and doesn't want to jump to conclusions.

But let's just say that it's fairly clear you have bipolar disorder. The mental health professional is relatively sure and so are you. What next? What can you expect?

treatment recommendations

Once a bipolar diagnosis has been established, the two most common treatment recommendations are currently psychotherapy and medication.

Psychotherapy

If your mental health professional is fairly certain that you've got bipolar disorder, then he or she will likely stress the importance of psychotherapy. If you haven't previously received any psychotherapy, you may wonder what it is. Simply put, it's the process of meeting with a mental health professional and talking about yourself in relation to what's occurring in your life. You may wonder, If bipolar disorder is mostly an illness of brain chemistry, then why would psychotherapy be so important?

The answer is simple: Coming to terms with your disorder and beginning to understand its impact upon you is essential. And because bipolar disorder affects your mind, it may be difficult to reflect on your own situation with clarity. A skilled psychotherapist can help you begin to look at how the disorder is affecting you and what kinds of adjustments are necessary so you can respond in an emotionally healthy way. We can almost guarantee that without that foundation in place, the rest of your treatment will be on shaky ground and future relapses will become more likely.

Psychotherapy will also help you manage your stress and untangle yourself from whatever situations are currently making your mood instability worse. Remember, high levels of stress can trigger mood instability, so you want to become good at stress management. But beyond management, good psychotherapy will help you to examine your life, look at your own recurring life patterns, and develop insight into your behavior.

Your sense of who you are, your self-esteem, and even your future aspirations are usually dealt a blow when you're diagnosed with bipolar disorder. It's like you suddenly feel you're no longer the person that you thought you were. If left unattended, this particular effect can set you up for future depression. Better to deal with it early in psychotherapy and reclaim your strengths, rather than try later, when you may be in the middle of dealing with acute depression.

Psychiatric Referral and Medications

If the clinician you see is a psychiatrist, he or she will likely suggest medication, and if not a psychiatrist, will refer you to one. In many ways a session with a psychiatrist that you've been referred to will be very similar to what you went through with the first clinician. Try not to become frustrated or discouraged with a second clinician's interview, even if this one covers the same territory as the first. Look at it as an opportunity for a second opinion. Often these interviews turn up new information or shed new light on old information that matters to your diagnosis and treatment.

Like the first therapist, the psychiatrist should reach a conclusion about whether you have a psychiatric disorder, and if so, which one. Don't be surprised if the psychiatrist recommends more than one medication. This may feel to you like rubbing salt in the wound. Perhaps you're thinking, "I must *really* be crazy." No, you're not crazy, but you may be bipolar. Bipolar disorder includes disturbances in brain chemistry that can result in multiple symptoms, so it only makes sense that it may need to be treated with multiple medications.

what's your role in this process?

When you go shopping for a car, you don't simply drive off with the first car you're shown. In fact, you may even visit many different lots or online sites. And most important, you'll ask many questions because you'll want to get a car that's just right for you. Well, the same applies to getting proper mental health treatment. You have the right to ask a lot of questions. Feel free to disagree if a mental health professional is sharing perceptions about you that you don't think are accurate. And more important, if you're being given treatment recommendations that don't feel right for you, speak up. The process of getting help is collaborative, and you and your mental health professional should be able to agree on a treatment approach that is acceptable to both of you. To assist you in preparing for a first appointment, we offer a set of questions that you may want to bring with you or review ahead of time.

questions for you to ask a mental health professional

- Can you tell me about your expertise in treating bipolar disorder? Approximately how many different bipolar patients have you treated?

- If you think I may be bipolar, what leads you to that conclusion?

- How certain do you feel about the diagnosis?

- Are there other diagnoses that you may also be considering?

- Why are you recommending these specific treatment approaches?

- With my medication, what can I anticipate? What side effects might I expect?

- How long should I expect to be on my specific medications?

- Who should I call if run into any trouble with my medicine or if I have any other unexpected emergencies?

- Are there alternative approaches I should be considering?

- What can you tell me about my prognosis?

- What are your thoughts about my receiving a second opinion?

- And anything else that feels important for you to know!

So there you have it: the initial phase of assessment. It's a big hump to get over. After all, we still live in an era when the reality of mental illness is marked by stigma. If you're bipolar, you may have to get used to that too. Societal attitudes change slowly, but it does appear that we're in the midst of significant change. Five to seven years ago you probably wouldn't have found a book like this. More and more people have better information and a better understanding about bipolar disorder. The future is promising, but you don't need to wait for the future to get help.

what you need to know about medications for bipolar disorder

From what we know, there is no way around this: if you have bipolar disorder, you will need to take medications. Most people aren't thrilled with taking medicine, but those who have had bad relapses of mania or depression will more easily accept the idea. It's like protecting your skin from the sun. Most of us don't want to put on sunscreen each time we go outside. If you've had a few bad sunburns, though, you're probably more open to the idea. We want to do everything possible to prevent you from suffering those mental sunburns.

Are You Really Crazy?

It's important to know that having bipolar disorder is very different from "being crazy." Crazy is not knowing what's real. Crazy is being out of control, possibly even dangerous. Crazy is hearing voices and often seeing things that aren't there. These experiences aren't totally out of the realm of possibility during an acute manic episode, but they are rare.

Many people with bipolar disorder lead very normal and productive lives. Most of the time your disorder will be invisible to others. The medications used to treat bipolar disorder can help keep it that way. These aren't drugs to be frightened of; they can make the difference between living a productive life and being on a roller coaster and feeling like you can't get off. But the medicines for bipolar disorder can have side effects, and some can be toxic if taken at levels that are too high. So it's appropriate to be cautious, and it's important to become educated about your medicine.

Do You Have to Worry About Getting Hooked on Meds?

You should also know that none of the drugs typically prescribed for bipolar disorder are addictive. You don't get high on them, nor will you become dependent on them, at least not in the typical sense that we think of when we consider drug dependency. In other words, if you find that you are prescribed medication and it helps you to manage your life more effectively, then you may come to "rely" upon your medicine to live a healthy life. This is basically is no different from the way a diabetic may rely upon insulin. The diabetic doesn't say, "I'm addicted to insulin." Addiction and the healthy use of medicine are radically different.

medications prescribed for bipolar disorder

The primary treatment for bipolar disorder is mood stabilizers. These are drugs that have antimanic and antidepressant actions. Different mood stabilizers are often used in combination. Some mood stabilizers are better at treating and preventing mania; others are better at treating and preventing recurrent depression. In this section, we'll take a tour of the most common drugs for bipolar, as these are the most likely to be an important part of your treatment. We anticipate new drug developments on the horizon, so stay informed through your mental health professionals and the media for the most current information on available medications.

Lithium

Although the term "mood stabilizer" is recent, the first mood stabilizer, lithium, was discovered to be effective in 1948. Lithium is toxic at high doses, so it has had a bad rap; however, at low doses it can give excellent results without side effects.

Although we don't know exactly how lithium works, we do know that it is effective in treating manic episodes and preventing the recurrence of mania. Additionally, it appears to have some antidepressant properties. Lithium is also the only drug known to actually reduce suicidal thoughts in people with bipolar disorder. Furthermore, recent evidence (Boku et al. 2009) suggests that low-dose use of lithium serves as "brain fertilizer," actually promoting the growth of neurons in the thinking, remembering, and feeling areas of the brain.

Anticonvulsants

For reasons that remain largely unknown, some of the same drugs effective in the treatment of epilepsy (*anticonvulsants*) also work in bipolar disorder. Because they also have mood stabilizing qualities, they've come to be known as mood stabilizers, especially when used to treat bipolar disorder. The table that follows describes the three mood stabilizing medications most commonly prescribed today. The trade name (given by the drug companies) is followed by the drug's generic name in parenthesis.

Commonly Prescribed Mood Stabilizers	
Depakote (valproate)	Promotes mellow feelings. Effective in treating acute mania, preventing migraines, and preventing recurrence of manic episodes.
Additional Comments	Increases the growth of your brain's gray matter and levels of substances that serve as "brain fertilizers." Blood levels need to be regularly monitored. Women of reproductive age risk possible development of ovarian cysts.
Lamictal (lamotrigine)	Works as an antidepressant and mood stabilizer. Helps to prevent relapses of depression.
Additional Comments	Is well tolerated with low risk of activating hypomania or mania. Also seems to be helpful to those who have rapid-cycling forms of bipolar disorder.
Tegretol (carbamazepine)	Reduces agitation. Its primary use is in acute mania and the prevention of manic relapses.
Additional Comments	Mostly prescribed to those prone to acute manic relapses.

Antipsychotics

An antipsychotic medication may also be prescribed. We appreciate that you probably don't like the name "antipsychotic" and all it may evoke. The word "psychotic" conjures up images of really crazy people in straitjackets. We wish there were a better name, such as resilience restorers, sane-itizers or mood mellowers. But for now we are stuck with the word, even though it hardly gives an idea of what these medications do. Antipsychotics were first developed to assist in the treatment of the most common psychotic illness, schizophrenia; however, their use has expanded much beyond schizophrenia. The original group of these drugs is called *typical antipsychotics* because despite their different names, they all do the same thing. Unfortunately, these drugs can produce side effects that look like Parkinson's disease: muscle rigidity and trouble walking. Partly because of their side effects, they were rarely used in treating patients with bipolar illness.

Atypical Antipsychotics

A new group of drugs, called *atypical antipsychotics*, has emerged in the last decade. These drugs do essentially the same thing as the earlier antipsychotics but have far fewer side effects. Soon after their introduction, the atypical antipsychotics were found to be effective in patients with bipolar disorder. While they are mostly used to help quiet mania and hypomania, they can also be effective in treating bipolar depression.

Like any effective medication, the atypical antipsychotics have side effects, including dizziness, sleepiness and fatigue, dry mouth, weight gain, and constipation. However, atypical antipsychotics in general are less likely to create Parkinson's-like symptoms. Geodon (ziprasidone) and Abilify (aripiprazole) can sometimes be too stimulating. You will want to review any potential side effects with your psychiatrist. If an antipsychotic drug is recommended, always ask for an atypical antipsychotic. They may cost more in dollars, but they'll have fewer costs in terms of comfort.

Commonly Prescribed Atypical Antipsychotics	
Abilify (aripiprazole)	One of the newer atypical antipsychotics. In addition to affecting areas of the brain responsible for emotion, it can also stimulate an area of the brain involved in attention and working memory.
Additional Comments	Known to help control emotion and enhance cognition simultaneously.
Geodon (ziprasidone)	Can quiet acute mania without the sedation caused by most other antipsychotics.
Additional Comments	Causes less or no weight gain and has fewer side effects.
Risperdal (risperidone)	Can be used effectively without triggering the side effects that look like Parkinson's disease symptoms.
Additional Comments	Is helpful with acute mania, long-term treatment, and perhaps even bipolar depression.
Seroquel (quetiapine)	Effective in quieting mania and agitation.
Additional Comments	May be particularly effective in treating the depressive aspects of bipolar disorder.
Zyprexa (olanzapine)	Calms agitation associated with severe mania and some forms of depression.
Additional Comments	Weight gain is a frequent side effect, and there is a risk for diabetes and elevated cholesterol levels.

if you're depressed, why can't you take an antidepressant?

Depression is a common part of the bipolar picture, yet routine use of antidepressants won't benefit you. It could even make things worse. The use of antidepressants in bipolar people leads to increased risk of hypomania or mania. When it's clear that you have bipolar disorder and you're currently in the midst of a depressive episode, mood stabilizing drugs are the safest treatment. What remains standard practice is to try an antidepressant only after one or more mood stabilizers are on board, because the mood stabilizers prevent the antidepressant from causing a manic episode. If you are prescribed an antidepressant, your response to the medication should be closely monitored by the prescribing physician. You don't want to end up in a hospital because of a manic episode triggered by your medication.

why you shouldn't stop your medications

You may reach a point when you think you can go without your medication. All of our patients have thought this. When your medications are working as they should and you're feeling much better, it's easy to think you no longer need them. Once you've stopped taking them and the side effects have faded away, you'll feel fine, which seems to be further evidence that life without medication is fine. Then, weeks later, you have another episode of hypomania, mania, depression, or all three, and you're back to where you started, or worse. We want to encourage you not to take this route.

Think of a factory that takes several weeks to produce its product. That's what your brain is: a factory that constantly produces neurotransmitters, their receptors, new nerve cells, "brain fertilizers," and much more. But the factory is slow. The drugs you take boost this factory's output of products. If you stop taking the drugs, the boost you started weeks ago is still moving through your system, independent of the drugs that started the process. This is how you're fooled into thinking you don't need the drugs. You've stopped them. You're free of any of the uncomfortable side effects that constantly served to remind you that you were taking medications in the first place. There's nothing that tells you that the medications' helpful effects are still working weeks after your last pill. You might even say, "Well, then I'll just stop taking my medication until I relapse, then go back on my meds until I'm feeling better. What's wrong with that?" Plenty!

Think of a sprained ankle. Every time you sprain your ankle, it makes that ankle a little weaker; it takes less force to cause another sprain. The brain is actually similar. We want to prevent relapses, not just to spare you from the suffering. Each time you relapse, you become more vulnerable to future episodes, more frequent episodes, more severe episodes, episodes resistant to medications, and episodes brought on by little or no stress. You don't want to go there. So, please, when you're feeling well and you're convinced you don't need medication, pause. Pick up this book. Find this chapter. Read this section again. Stay on your medications and consult with your psychiatrist!

CHAPTER THREE

how do you accept all this?

When you first have a sense that something's wrong psychologically, you probably don't want to face it. In fact, it's much easier to gently push it away and hope that it's just a fluke. Often this works because unexpected things do occur and they're not necessarily part of a broader pattern. But when you're dealing with the initial symptoms of a mood disorder, trying to ignore these signs could make things worse.

→ Ashley's story

Ashley had it pretty good up to age seventeen. Not that life was perfect, but so far there hadn't been any major trauma. She found life full of possibilities. She loved music and art, and her teachers assured her that she was gifted.

By early spring of her junior year, Ashley's creative energy blazed up with newfound strength. She frequently found herself painting into the early morning hours, and she was excited that she could do so with little impact on her daily life. Colors were alive with intensity and each painting spawned another. The artistic possibilities seemed endless, while the boring, ordinary obligations of homework and going to class seemed increasingly pointless.

After about two weeks her parents realized that this new behavior was not just a passing phase. Ashley was consumed by her painting and it seemed to be the only thing she wanted to discuss. Her speech was becoming increasingly rapid and intense. This was not the soft-spoken Ashley that her parents were used to, and the changes truly concerned them. They began talking to Ashley about getting help, but she only became more defiant in response to these discussions, insisting that she had all the time she needed to attend to her schoolwork—and she believed it too. In fact, she thought she could do just about anything if she put her mind to it. Ashley was excited. She felt better than ever. But her parents were worried. They hadn't seen their child quite like this before.

In another couple of weeks, things really unraveled. Ashley's thoughts were coming so fast, and the intensity of the colors in her painting was so distracting, that it was difficult for her to create a piece that was anything but visual chaos. At one point her physical energy became so immense she felt she was close to exploding. It seemed her only viable option was to run through the house screaming, desperately hoping she could dispel some of the pressure that was overwhelming her. But she couldn't. It all became a nightmarish blur: the police...the ambulance...her mother's crying...the physical restraints...being admitted to the hospital's psych unit at 3 a.m.

As the injected drugs began to take over, Ashley felt like something had flattened her brain. She couldn't think or easily talk. She stayed in this flattened state for several days, a kind of suspended animation. Eventually the antipsychotic medication was reduced and a mood stabilizer added. During a meeting with her parents and her psychiatrist, she was told she had bipolar disorder. She would remain in the hospital for another couple of days and then return home to some of the routines of her life.

Life did sort of return to normal: school, friends, band practice, and dinnertime with family. An added new element was her weekly visits with Dr. Bradley. She liked Dr. Bradley. She was easy to talk to and Ashley frequently came away from her sessions feeling more normal. But each week there was a portion of their time devoted to a talk about the medication and the importance of Ashley's continuing its use. Dr. Bradley assured her that she would likely be able to remain stable and continue on with most aspects of her life as long as she took her medication and made sure that she kept a regular sleep schedule.

By the end of the school year, Ashley felt like she was gradually coming to terms with this thing called bipolar disorder, although for the most part the diagnosis remained pretty much a secret. Apart from her school guidance counselor, a few teachers, and her family, no one else knew about her breakdown and the hospitalization. She told her friends she had been home with a bad case of the flu.

From time to time she wanted to be able to share what she was going through, but the prospect of telling anyone was scary. Would people think she was crazy? Would guys stay away? Would families in her neighborhood stop trusting her to babysit? Despite all she had read online about bipolar disorder, she still hoped it would gradually disappear and she would someday return to her normal self without the craziness ever being exposed.

So she tried hard to "be good" and do as she was told and, in many respects, this worked. But try as she did, she couldn't find her way back into painting. Sure, the form and proportion on canvas were still good. She certainly knew how to mix colors. But there was something about her creative energy that she could no longer connect with. She tried switching from oil paints to acrylics. She tried painting in the morning instead of at night. With Dr. Bradley's permission, she even tried discontinuing the low-dose antipsychotic that she took before bedtime. But nothing did the trick. It was like the drugs had taken something away and she couldn't figure out how to find her way back to the passion she had enjoyed.

Without this specific quality of creativity, everything else that was positive in Ashley's life felt like it didn't matter. She gradually became depressed and sapped of energy. For the first time, she found herself flirting with thoughts of suicide. Dr. Bradley prescribed some antidepressant medication, which sort of helped. At least the depression lifted. But the flatness and the absence of creative juice remained the same. Ashley would look at pieces she had done only six months earlier and feel like she was looking at artwork created by a stranger.

By early in her senior year she was struggling with the reality of upcoming university applications. During the Christmas break of her junior year, she and her family had visited several universities with strong fine arts programs. She had always known art wasn't a very practical choice, though her parents had nurtured her artistic desires and had affirmed that pursuing one's passions was more important than forgoing them to make money. But without passions to pursue, how was she going to choose her school? If not art school, then what else?

Six months after her hospitalization, Ashley's sessions with Dr. Bradley were reduced to once per month. The discussions about medication were less frequent, and Ashley's own routine with her medication had become a bit looser. To her surprise, she found that if she skipped her meds for a day or two, she really felt no differently. And with this realization, the periods of time without medication became more purposeful, more frequent, and delightfully without any negative consequence.

It was time for the grand experiment. Ashley first took herself off the antidepressant, finding clear instructions as to how to manage this from a simple Google search. She then went off of her mood stabilizer, also approaching the task conscientiously—or at least so she thought. And as for her next visit with Dr. Bradley, it was just like the last one, with Ashley assuring Dr. Bradley that she was grateful for the benefit she found from her medication. This same deception also worked with her parents.

Little by little, Ashley's painting exuberance returned. Although her sense of excitement and rebirth came none too soon, she also had a fair amount of catching up to do in preparing her application portfolio. However, without Dr. Bradley's assistance Ashley felt cautious, almost hypervigilant, with regard to her mood and energy. She didn't want to blow it and return to the craziness of last spring.

Toward the end of fall in her senior year, Ashley felt way too stretched. There was too much to do and not enough time to get it all done. Increasingly she felt bouts of energy. And while she enjoyed her productivity during these periods, she was also aware that she was playing with fire. On the nights she couldn't sleep, she would rely on cough medicine or alcohol to help quiet things down. But what she couldn't quiet down, even in her dreams, was a growing sense of agitation and urgency. Getting into art school became an all-consuming, nonnegotiable goal. Plus, she would only consider applying to the nation's top-rated fine arts programs, ignoring the important advice to apply to at least one safe school that she could be sure of getting into.

By early January Ashley had finally submitted her four applications. Instead of feeling relieved, though, she felt tied up in knots. All she could do now was wait to see if her efforts had been enough. The intensity felt familiar, though not out of control or noticeable by others. But unlike last spring, it now felt more frightening. Ashley's memory of the hospital was all too clear as she desperately tried to hold on to stability without letting on just how shaky everything felt.

In mid-February Ashley received her first rejection letter, two weeks later the second, and by mid-March, two more. She crashed hard. She wasn't able to tone down her sense of failure and inadequacy, and her thoughts had developed a harsh, angry, self-punishing edge. She knew she could no longer keep a lid on her agitation, and she also knew she had no recourse but to face the extent to which she had screwed up. Less than a week after the last rejection letter, Ashley's parents found her in a pool of blood on the bathroom floor with both wrists cut deeply. By the time she arrived at the hospital she was close to death. When she eventually regained consciousness in the intensive care unit, she once again felt flattened, though this time it was not from drugs, but from the recognition that she was still here, along with her bipolar disorder.

Everyone with bipolar disorder has his or her own story, and no two are the same. When listening to people share stories about their bipolar experience, we do begin to hear some recurrent themes. One that stands out with Ashley is her sense of something being wrong but not wanting to face it.

the stigma of mental illness

It's one thing to get sick or injured; just think of the sore throats or slight illnesses you've had in the past. With these occurrences, you feel a little bit bummed, but you also recognize that these are just the passing realities of being human. The same doesn't apply to mental illness. Certainly there are times when you come up against limitations in brain power. You may wish you could read faster or remember more or calculate better or be a whiz at learning a foreign language. While you may want to be smarter, generally you do just fine. Even when you feel intellectually challenged, most of the time you don't feel like something's wrong with you, and you don't assume that you'll be vulnerable to mental illness; that's something that happens to other people, not you.

Bipolar disorder expresses itself with as much variability as the people who have it. The many faces of bipolar disorder also have many different phases. You might recognize that years before you ever had your first manic episode, there were times when you felt like you were on a moderate-sized emotional roller coaster. No one diagnosed you as being sick. But it wouldn't have surprised you to be told that you were moody or to hear a comment like "You're always so intense."

defensiveness in response to feedback: a common reaction

When you hear something like "You're always so intense," you may interpret it as some sort of negative judgment. It would seem that these kinds of comments or perceptions, when translated into straight talk, really mean "You're difficult to deal with" or "Sometimes you can be a pain in the ass." This just isn't the same as someone saying, "You seem to have a cold" or "I see you've sprained your ankle." The most common reaction when you feel criticized is to put up a defensive wall in an attempt to protect yourself from feeling hurt.

The wall doesn't always work. Comments about your moodiness usually do hurt. But the wall also gets in the way of objectively considering the reality of what someone else may be saying. When you hear others say, "You're moody," "You're difficult to deal with," or other variations on that theme, how often do you stop and think to yourself, "Am I really difficult? Am I different from my friends? Could my moodiness be abnormal?" Well, unless you've been diagnosed for quite a while and you're familiar with the different warning signs that let you know you're entering a period of instability, comments from others often don't shed any light.

And then, another important factor gets in the way of acknowledging something's wrong. To objectively assess your feelings requires some mental juggling. It requires you to interrupt your immersion in your experience and take a step outside to look inward. This is easier said than done, especially when your emotional reactions are strong. For example, when you're angry you may find it hard to step outside of the anger and reflect upon it, where it comes from, whether or not it's justified, and whether it's out of proportion with the situation. It's much easier to do this after you've calmed down. Being successful with these mental gymnastics in the middle of intense emotion can be difficult. That's true for everyone, not just for those who are bipolar.

When you're bipolar, though, even before the disorder fully emerges your emotions seem to have more dynamism, like when Ashley became drawn into her artwork with all her passion. She didn't think, "It's odd that the colors seem so vivid or that my painting feels so urgent." She just felt it. And the more she felt it, the more she felt drawn into her pleasurable experience. In the first few weeks, before things got out of hand, Ashley might have said, "Being me right now feels great." That's very characteristic of what we described in chapter 2 as hypomania. Hypomania comes along and says, "Hey, follow me; let's go have some fun." You don't feel like there is anything wrong, so you run with it, just like Ashley did.

In the second part of Ashley's story, when she came off her medication, she felt good at first. Her thoughts seemed clear. Her actions were goal directed. She felt committed to her college applications. She also felt good to be off her medication. For a brief period of time she was able to get away from the painful reminder that swallowing a mood stabilizer a couple of times daily meant that she was bipolar. What a relief!

As weeks became months, Ashley's experience changed. There was an edge, a sense of desperation, a feeling of not being able to relax. She also felt guilty about lying and fearful that things would come crashing down again. She couldn't easily calm herself, and this was frightening. The memories of her previous emotional crash were still fresh. And what made all of it even more frightening was the agitated energy that she was beginning to feel. It was pushing and she couldn't push back. The same was true just before her first hospitalization. When she ran through her house screaming, she had no choice; in the midst of full mania, she was so consumed by it that she had no ability to stop and realize what she was doing.

not wanting to accept your bipolar reality

When we return to Ashley's experience during her college application process, we see that she knew something was happening that she really didn't want to accept. If she had been honest with herself or her psychiatrist, she probably would have said something like "I have a feeling that something's wrong, but I don't want to admit it." And the reason she didn't want to admit it is painfully clear: She didn't want to be bipolar. She didn't want to have to take medication. She didn't want to accept the effect of medication on her creativity. She didn't want to face the impact her disorder and the medication might have on her future. She didn't want to be different from other people. She desperately wanted to be able to return to her old self, and she couldn't find her way back. Who would want any of that? Not Ashley, not you, not anyone.

There are parts of being bipolar you can't accept because you're immersed in it and you can't see it. There are parts of being bipolar that you don't want to accept because doing so feels like you're different, broken, or defective. And there are parts of being bipolar that are difficult to accept because the long-term implications are hard to make peace with.

Ashley's second time heading toward instability was a painful reminder of the first. What if it were her third or fifth or ninth? There's a point where the onset of symptoms becomes a painful reminder of that dreaded part of life, a familiar but unwelcome visitor. Until you reach the point where you can truly accept the disorder without feeling overwhelmed by the fear and anger and loss, all you want to do is run from it. These feelings are normal and understandable. They are even predictable. Most people with bipolar disorder struggle with such feelings during the early stages of the journey.

vulnerability: an unfamiliar aspect of the emerging self

The bipolar diagnosis brings another challenge into play during late adolescence and early adulthood: the feeling of being defective. Most likely, you're not prepared for the sense of vulnerability that's involved.

When you were a child, the adult world felt far off. You were little; the adults were big. You were dependent; they were in control. There was a lot about the world that was a mystery to you but not to them. Clearly, their place in the world was really different from yours.

Once through high school, you probably begin to recognize that the next phase of your life really is the early part of being a "grown-up." For some, college and graduate school are the early parts of a longer-range trajectory. For others, the first full-time job out of high school is the first step in finding a career. And even if you don't have a clear vision about your future, you still know that the phase of your life between seventeen and twenty-five is about preparing for adulthood. Ideally, it feels like it's the beginning of a long-term progression.

Given that this part of life is all about preparation, it isn't a time when most people are focused upon their limitations and vulnerabilities. That's not to say that during your teens or early twenties you don't feel a lot of insecurities. Of course you do; it's an integral part of being young. But this is also a time when you and the adults involved with you are trying to mobilize your strengths and develop your capacities in many different aspects of your life. It's like you're in basic training for adulthood. It's a time of growth and learning, a time to strive and reach. It's a time when you're often looking forward and wondering, "What's next?"

When things do go wrong, it's a real shock. If you've experienced the sudden death of a parent, sibling, or close friend, just think how the experience knocked you over. There's not much in life that helps us prepare for the death of a loved one. We only get better at accepting tragedy through experience, and gaining that experience—well, it sucks. The same holds true for other kinds of vulnerability, sickness being the most commonly shared one. When you're fifty, you might begin to think about things like cancer or heart disease; when you're twenty these seem like mere words, not something to fear.

When you get into a car to drive to a friend's, you almost never think you may not get where you're going; you just assume it's a done deal. But sometimes people don't get where they're going. And when you hear about a friend's death from an auto accident, you can't believe it. The same holds for death from disease, or for the development of a chronic illness or injury that changes a person's life. Just imagine becoming a paraplegic as a result of an accident, or facing cancer as a teenager, or developing diabetes and having to cope with all the long-term implications of being insulin-dependent. The point is, you're at a place where these kinds of realities just don't seem probable. Unless you've struggled with trauma or numerous tragedies or illnesses during childhood, you probably have a sense of invulnerability during this stage of your life. It's not abnormal; you simply haven't yet gone through the phases of life when human vulnerability and fragility are likely to be a big part of your experience.

The reality of bipolar disorder is no different from an accident, cancer, or diabetes. Being diagnosed with bipolar means you go through a progression from feeling like a normal person to feeling like something's not right. You struggle with it on your own for a while. You eventually tell someone else. You seek help and you receive the diagnosis. If you take medication that helps to smooth things out, that's great, but you still know that the disorder hasn't gone away. It's hibernating and you don't want to wake it up. The reality is hard to believe, especially when you're on the front end of it. It's even harder to accept. It doesn't fit with your sense of who you are. And if you really let that reality into your head, then your sense of invulnerability has been changed for good.

wanting to fit in

One of the hardest things about being bipolar is that most of the world is not. You truly are in a minority: approximately 2 percent of the population. None of us like to stand out in any way that seems abnormal. It's cool to be known as smart, funny, or attractive. It's not cool to be known as unstable, moody, or bipolar. Essentially, bipolar is seen in our culture as a kind of defect. Now, admittedly, this view is changing. More and more, we're finding that celebrities and other well-known public figures are acknowledging that they have bipolar disorder. It's even commonly associated with artistic creativity. So when you learn that a famous painter, musician, or playwright is bipolar, it may not come as such a surprise. But just imagine the scenario of having someone who is bipolar run for president of the United States. It simply wouldn't happen in this day and age. In fact, it may not ever happen because of the unpredictability of relapse into periods of instability.

Most of us don't aspire to be president, but almost all of us want to fit in and be accepted. During your teens and early twenties, wanting to fit in is a common experience. You want people to like you; you want to be included. It may be that the pressures to fit in, to be popular, and to belong to a group—any group—are stronger during this time than during any other period in your life.

Because fitting in and being accepted are important, accepting anything about yourself that's quite different from others becomes an enormous challenge. If you find that your mood has a negative impact on the way you act, then it poses a big risk to your sense of confidence about fitting in. You don't want to be walking around with the identity of being the bipolar kid on campus, and most likely you'll want to conceal it, at least until you've become more comfortable with it yourself.

But here's the dilemma: When you're in the middle of your intense moods, you don't necessarily have the option of easily controlling them. Ashley tried by drinking alcohol, a common strategy that people think will help them chill. Mental health professionals call it *self-medication*. Unfortunately, it doesn't work because, rather than helping you to hide or squash your intensity, alcohol breaks down your inhibitions, making everything tend to flow outward more freely. Whether because of alcohol or simply because of your own uncontrolled emerging self, parts of the bipolar picture are eventually going to be noticed by others.

You can always try denying or concealing it: "Oh, there's nothing wrong. I'm just having a bad day" or "Sometimes I do get really excited, but it's no big deal. My whole family is this way." These kinds of brief deflections work only if others don't see you that often. But when someone is around you a lot, like a roommate or a close friend, then over time the pattern of your high and low moods will become evident and your denial of the experience won't hold water for long.

Finally the cat's out of the bag. Usually this can be pretty scary, and you may be flooded with questions: What will others think? Will they still want to be around me? Will they feel like they have to handle me with kid gloves? Will they be scared of handling me at all? If I'm laughing and having a great time, will they just think I'm being manic? If I'm down and depressed, will they worry about me? Will anything be the same once they know?

It's hard to answer these questions with certainty. Partly the answers depend on the extent of your symptoms and how well the people around you understand them. If you become too emotionally expressive, then some people may back away. If you're admitted to a psychiatric hospital, it's not likely that many will visit. If you were in the hospital because of an accident, your friends would want to visit you. But if you're on a psychiatric unit, it's just not the same. They may not have a clue as to how to relate to you. Now you're not just a friend; you're a friend with a mental disorder.

The reality is that bipolar disorder can have a huge impact on your social life. It can end a relationship. It can impulsively start one. It can wear other people out. It can scare them away. It can do all of the above—and more. Now we don't mean to paint a bleak picture. In fact, how well you manage your life with bipolar disorder will make a huge difference in your social relationships. We'll talk in the next chapter about how to live a successful life with bipolar. But for now, our intent is to let you know that the symptoms of the disorder will very likely have some degree of impact upon your interpersonal world.

Will you ever get to a place where you can simply be comfortable enough with others to freely share this secret? Some people do, some don't, and there are a lot of people with bipolar who fall somewhere in between. It's only after you've lived with bipolar disorder for a while that you become comfortable enough with its reality to begin to disclose your diagnosis to others. There may be others you want to tell about your illness beyond your immediate family, but for the most part, the initial process of self-disclosure is often tentative and gradual. That's normal. It probably reflects good judgment. It's okay to take your time with it and very gradually see how things unfold. The bottom line is that being bipolar complicates your social life, and it's one more reason why accepting the diagnosis is difficult.

the inevitable tendency toward denial

In the previous section we spoke about the desire not to have others view you as bipolar. That's a pretty simple concept. Most things that cause us to feel embarrassed or ashamed also lead us to try to hide those things from others. But there's an aspect of denial in relation to bipolar disorder that's harder to grasp. We're talking about the experience of trying to deny something within your own mind—essentially trying to take your awareness of your bipolar disorder and erase it or somehow make it disappear because you don't want it there.

The Power and Protection of Denial

Denial is a powerful defense when it works. It's really an amazing mental maneuver when you think about it: we can take our awareness of something and cancel it out through a series of mental processes, some of which happen outside our conscious awareness.

Think about the experience of doing poorly in a class. If you know several other classmates who are also not doing well, it then becomes easy to see them as an extension of the whole class and to conclude that everyone's struggling. This also makes it the teacher's responsibility rather than yours, so you don't have to feel your own sense of failure. The denial sounds something like "Yeah, that course is really tough and the teacher just doesn't know how to get the material across." This conclusion is very different from

"I got a D because I didn't study enough." You see, the others who did poorly also haven't studied adequately. The denial doesn't take into account the fact that 25 percent of the class received A's.

So denial provides temporary relief. It protects us from facing anything that is difficult to accept, but it doesn't work as a long-term defense. At some point reality usually catches up to us. When it does, the implications are usually more painful and more consequential than if we had simply faced reality in the first place. So why do we do it? Simply, it postpones the process of coming to terms with something that's unwanted.

→ Jason

Jason graduated from college with a bright future in engineering. He accepted a position with a top-notch architectural engineering firm. While he hadn't previously worked on an actual architectural site, he was convinced he was bright enough and that his course work had adequately prepared him to handle the job.

Within the first couple of months he was the company's new shining star. He would often stay at work late into the night, plowing through pages of architectural plans, computing stress loads, and doing many other calculations in order to determine what kinds of materials needed to be used for the construction. Sometimes he only got two or three hours of sleep or even worked all night, but this seemed to be of little concern for him. It was much more important to Jason that he get the job done and prove his worth to his new employer. His recommendations were on the money, and the company was more than pleased with their new hire.

After a while Jason found that during team meetings it was difficult for him to listen to others without taking a dominant role in the discussion. He was convinced his approach was superior, and he couldn't easily be open to alternative strategies. He found that once he became caught up in discussion, it was difficult for him to stop and allow others equal airtime. Some of his coworkers were getting irritated with his pushiness, though his immediate supervisor was more concerned about Jason's behavior and his apparent lack of sleep. The supervisor just happened to be familiar with bipolar disorder and he suggested Jason see a shrink. Jason thought this was ludicrous but decided to comply out of respect for his supervisor. Besides, this job was important enough to him that he didn't want to convey the impression of being an uncooperative employee.

The shrink seemed nice enough, and after obtaining a more extensive family history from Jason, including that an uncle was bipolar and Jason's mother was depressed, the psychiatrist informed Jason that he might possibly be experiencing the initial phase of bipolar disorder.

He recommended that Jason try a mood stabilizer. Again, Jason thought this was uncalled for, but he decided to go along with the recommendation. At some level that he wasn't totally aware of, Jason also believed the psychiatrist might be right. After all, Jason might have been going through some denial, but he wasn't stupid. He had heard about bipolar and he knew his own family history could be a contributing factor.

To his surprise, he felt better over the next couple of months. His sleep cycle smoothed out. He was less driven at work and his relationships with his colleagues seemed to improve. Jason continued to do well, and he saw his success as evidence that his psychiatrist's notion about bipolar disorder was way off base. It didn't occur to him that he might be doing well because the medication was helping.

After about four months, Jason stopped his medication and canceled his appointments with his shrink. He felt fine and didn't think he needed treatment. He continued to be effective at work, which provided further confirmation of his theory that the whole bipolar thing was clearly a misdiagnosis.

Near the end of his first year with the company, Jason received some less than glowing feedback due to recent work that wasn't quite up to par. Mind you, it wasn't bad; it just wasn't the kind of feedback he was used to.

Jason couldn't shake the negative feeling he was left with, and he gradually slid into a depressive funk. After weeks of feeling like he was slogging his way through his days, he finally sought help again with someone new. Only this time, when he discussed his depression he decided not to mention his previous hypomanic episode or his previous course of treatment with a mood stabilizer. He didn't want the psychiatrist to jump on the bipolar bandwagon. He wanted a quick fix for his depression, and he was hoping he could leave the bipolar stuff behind.

His new psychiatrist prescribed one of the more frequently used antidepressants without having accurate information about Jason's psychiatric history. Within a week's time, Jason spiked into a full manic episode. He was truly out of control at work. He was quite frightening to everyone he came into contact with and landed in a psychiatric hospital for two weeks. His diagnosis was bipolar I disorder. Much like Ashley, Jason learned the hard way that he couldn't leave it behind.

Jason's story could apply to many people with bipolar. We've found that denial plays out more frequently with bipolar disorder than with many other psychiatric issues. If you're anxious, you're usually not in denial about it. The anxiety grabs you and rigorously shakes you. You know all too well that you're being shaken. If you're struggling with trauma, you know that you're always feeling on edge. Your flashbacks are frightening, and a lot of different experiences in life seem to precipitate rapid emotional changes. Similarly, depression pulls you down and you know you're being pulled down. You feel bad, sad, and unmotivated, and usually your perception of yourself is pretty low.

the bipolar masquerade

Bipolar is a different kind of animal. Almost two-thirds of the bipolar experience can masquerade as something other than bipolar illness. The hypomanic aspects can sneak up on you with such stealth that you don't even recognize their presence. They just feel like they're a part of you, maybe even a new and improved you. So why would you think anything was wrong?

If you're bipolar, you may have extended periods of time when your mood is stable. This stability can be a result of your medication doing what it's supposed to, or it may be that you're fortunate enough to be in a quiet and stable phase, unmedicated and feeling normal. If that's the case, wouldn't you naturally say, "Things are good, and I'm feeling fine"? Of course you would. And if your own denial about the disorder is kicking in, it's so much easier to be in the present than to be focused on your broader behavioral patterns.

Wouldn't the depressive side of being bipolar pull you out of denial? Maybe, but not necessarily. It's true that depression feels awful. But you can always blame your depression on the bad things that happen to you. When things go wrong, you feel bad, and if you experience a series of negative events, it makes sense that you'd feel bad for a while. Therefore, it's easy to see depression as a normal reaction to life rather than attributing it to bipolar disorder.

What makes it easier for depression and denial to interact together is that with more acute phases of depression, a person's thinking actually becomes dulled. It's like twenty points are knocked off of your IQ, so your ability to be sharp and clear about what's going on becomes impaired. You feel awful. You're not necessarily thinking clearly about your varying mood swings.

When you're down, you're down. When you're up, you're seduced by the pleasure. When you're stable, you're relieved that you're not unstable. And at any point on this continuum, you probably don't want to see the whole picture because it's a painful and difficult one to see.

Denial is an important aspect of bipolar illness. It may very well affect you, but you won't know it, at least not if it works, because when it works, seeing yourself objectively becomes really difficult. That usually requires help—from friends, family, loved ones, and probably from mental health professionals. In chapter 5 we will address how to take advantage of these resources and accompanying strategies. The important piece here is that to get out of denial, you will probably need help from others. Trying to go it alone with bipolar disorder isn't a very successful strategy.

anger and helplessness: the precursors of depression

Being bipolar carries with it certain emotions that are common, especially for people in the early phases of dealing with the illness. Anger and helplessness are two of the big ones. We don't mean that becoming angry with others is common, although if your relationships with others involve some strong conflicts, then anger at them may be one by-product. We're talking more about the experience of feeling angry at your disorder. After all, it's there and it's been diagnosed. But you can't argue with it. You can't hit it. You can't throw it away. You can't engage it in battle and conquer it. Basically, you feel like this thing has occupied your mind and you're stuck with it. Though you can try to manage the effects of the disorder, you can't really make it go away. So you feel both angry and helpless. Unless you can accept these feelings and learn how to handle them, you're likely to feel tripped up whenever they're present. Let's separate out these two sets of emotions and focus first upon the anger.

Being Angry at Your Disorder

Think back to when you first learned you were bipolar or when you first suspected you might be. You may have had the quite common reaction of rejection or disbelief: "There must be some mistake!" If those reactions go on for a while, then you become caught up in the denial and resistance that we discussed in the previous section. But if you seek out professional help, then you're going to hear a lot of things about managing your disorder. Some of what you hear will give you hope that living with bipolar disorder holds many possibilities for a life of satisfaction and fulfillment; however, there will be other professional advice that isn't all that exciting or pleasurable. A partial list would look like this:

- The medication may have side effects such as drowsiness, upset stomach, dry mouth, headache, dizziness, a sense of being emotionally or cognitively dulled, decreased sexual desire, and difficulties having orgasm.

- Assuming your psychiatrist prescribes medication that's a good fit for you but you stop using it, you increase the likelihood of a relapse—that is, another bipolar episode.

- Depending upon what medication you're prescribed, you may need to have your blood drawn and tested regularly.

- You need to consistently get enough sleep. If you don't, you may be at risk of another period of instability.

- You need to refrain from the use of psychoactive substances such as alcohol or pot.

- You'll benefit from attending psychotherapy sessions on a regular basis.

- You probably shouldn't travel in regions of the world where you don't have easy access to psychiatric services. This means that about three-quarters of the world is off-limits to you.

- Even if you do all the above, you're not guaranteed continued stability.

- Bipolar disorder does have a genetic basis, and you face increased odds that your children or grandchildren may be affected by the disorder.

We assume that this list doesn't reflect what you truly want for your life. In fact, just reading the list may make you feel angry. It's like there's this broad range of "shoulds" that you've got to deal with now and in the years to come, and most of it doesn't fit with your current lifestyle.

Why wouldn't you feel angry when, just like Ashley, you have a hard time connecting with your creative energy? Or when, like Jason, just when you think you've overcome the disorder, your manic symptoms rapidly emerge and knock you on your butt? Consider the frustration of having to end a great time with friends at 11:30 p.m. in order to go home and get to sleep. Or worse, you're on a first date and you're both really hitting it off. You think to yourself, "Damn, this could really lead to something!" Then comes all the complexity of being bipolar.

Yes, all these changes that bipolar disorder imposes can really feel like a big wrench is being thrown into the middle of your life and your relationships. And what makes this even more difficult is that bipolar often arrives on the scene at a time when the changes it requires are the complete opposite of what's normal at that time of life.

If you're in your late teens or early twenties, you're beginning to separate from your parents and you're building a life of your own. And if you're not quite there yet, you're certainly looking forward to it. Making choices such as not staying up too late, not drinking or getting high, not traveling to far-off destinations, and seeing a shrink on a regular basis may all feel painfully limiting, as if you're going in reverse. You've finally reached the point where you're ready to stretch your wings and fly, and instead you have to contend with realities that keep you tethered to the ground.

Maybe anger is an understatement. How about rage? How about wanting to rant about the unfairness of life? How about more? But here's the kicker: Usually if you're frustrated with specific problems of life and you can channel your anger into constructive efforts to change something, then change can be a realistic possibility. But this doesn't work with bipolar disorder. While you can do everything possible to live a productive and satisfying life with bipolar disorder, you can't transform your life into one without the disorder. And so follow the feelings of helplessness.

Helplessness: The Other Side of the Coin

Helplessness is what you feel when your hopes, desires, and efforts to change something consistently meet with failure. This isn't a feeling that people typically welcome. Helplessness is often what comes before depression.

Helplessness doesn't happen in isolation. In fact, there's often a recurring sequence of emotions that takes you into the experience of helplessness and then into depression. At first you become frustrated and angry that you can't influence a situation, but fueled by your anger, you keep trying. And if you're really motivated, you may even press on well past the point where you see that your efforts aren't being successful. Once the anger peters out, you're likely to give up and lapse into the experience of helplessness. And if you combine your experience of helplessness with the perception that getting cured of the bipolar disorder will never happen, then you've got the recipe for clinical depression.

Anger and helplessness at bipolar disorder are two sides of the same coin. They're experiences that you will visit frequently, especially at the start of the bipolar journey. As much as you might like to skip over this part of the journey, it's pretty much inevitable. You have a choice: you can desperately hold on to your denial in order to hold your bipolar reality at bay, or you can do your best to face the feelings of anger and helplessness that you're inevitably going to encounter if you're bipolar. Our strong advice is that you focus most of your energies on the latter.

pseudo-acceptance: a common blind spot

You may be one of those people who always tries to do the right thing. It's how you've been raised. It's how you live your life. If that fits, then you may find that you don't connect at all with a desire to reject your diagnosis. You get help. You take your meds, and you seem to adjust well. You seem to have accepted the reality of bipolar disorder, but possibly you have only masked or denied your deeper, more complex feelings about the illness.

→ Marcia's Story

Marcia came from a family where mood disorders were not uncommon. Her maternal grandfather was very emotionally unstable, though he was never diagnosed or treated. Her mother had been diagnosed with manic depression in her midtwenties, and Marcia's childhood memories were colored by her mother's intense emotionality, interrupted by periods of time when her mother was in the hospital. Marcia's older brother had a stormy adolescence that transitioned into a predominant depression from his late teens. He had been treated with several different antidepressants and his physician finally found one that seemed to be effective, but generally speaking he did not live a happy life.

Marcia's father had left the family when she was about six. He wasn't prepared to deal with his wife's problems, nor was he ready to be both mother and father to his two children.

It's no surprise that Marcia had always lived with fears of becoming bipolar, and that every small dip or elevation in her mood seemed a threat of something bigger.

Marcia experienced her first full-blown manic episode during her junior year in college. Her symptoms were classic, though she also experienced delusions in which she was convinced that she had some rare, undiagnosable disease. She was hospitalized and placed on a mood stabilizer as well as antipsychotic medication. The latter was prescribed to clear up the delusions.

Marcia's symptoms resolved after about six days of hospitalization, and she was again feeling like her old self. Despite some mild side effects from the medicine, her mania and subsequent hospitalization were actually a relief, as she was no longer walking on eggshells waiting for trouble.

Marcia had been a biology major, and before her hospitalization she had her heart set on becoming a physical therapist. In fact, she had already selected four different master's programs in physical therapy where she was going to apply during her next semester.

From her psychiatrist's perspective, Marcia was the ideal patient. She had cooperated with all treatment recommendations and had rapidly embraced the reality of the diagnosis. Given her mother's diagnosis, Marcia had already read extensively about this illness. She was a walking Wikipedia when it came to the many different aspects of bipolar disorder.

During the summer after her junior year, Marcia made a significant shift in her long-range career plans. She decided that she wanted to learn more about psychiatric conditions and dedicate her life to working with others who struggled with psychiatric disorders. She identified several programs where she could obtain a nursing degree while also progressing toward a master's in psychiatric nursing. The plan felt exciting to her and provided a meaningful direction. She was sure that her own life experience would help her be effective as a psychiatric professional.

Marcia did everything by the book. She was very conscientious about sleep. She never missed her medication. She tolerated the side effects of her drugs by simply telling herself they were a necessary consequence of treatment. She was open about her bipolar disorder and readily informed any love interest about her condition. Sadly, Marcia's efforts at finding a love relationship didn't pan out; while she had several friends, her deep yearning for a strong, stable, and lasting intimate relationship remained unfulfilled.

Marcia had little difficulty being accepted to the school of her choice, and her first two years of course work went quite well. It was also noteworthy that she had remained very stable since the onset of her disorder.

During Marcia's first set of clinical rotations, she found she was having racing thoughts with increasing irritability. It was especially noticeable when she was at a nursing facility with elderly patients. Quite uncharacteristically, Marcia had little patience for the verbal rambling of her patients with dementia. She knew something wasn't right, so she scheduled a session with her psychiatrist, who increased the dose of her current medication.

Unfortunately, the stronger dose didn't adequately apply the brakes, and one day Marcia exploded at a frail eighty-three-year-old woman who was relating to her as if she were the woman's own daughter. Marcia's blowup was clearly inappropriate, but the real problem was that the explosions continued and she wound up back in the hospital for a second time. She kept trying to tell herself that she was only experiencing a brief period of instability. But her rational defense didn't work against her intense emotional outbursts.

This hospitalization was very different from the first time. Her psychiatrist tried some different medications that seemed to help with her manic symptoms. But once her mania was under control she spiraled downward into an agitated depression. Rather than a set of classic manic symptoms being affected by psychotic distortion, her emotions seemed much more connected to her core issues. She was angry with the hospital staff because she thought they weren't sensitive to her needs. She was angry at her mother's bipolar disorder for robbing her of a normal childhood. She felt hopeless about the prospects of ever being "normal," and she felt both anger and despair over not being able to change any of it. This wasn't just agitated depression; it was a whole lifetime of unresolved conflicts and unfulfilled needs.

Marcia was discharged after about a week, but her intense emotions didn't quickly resolve with new medications. Instead, it took months of twice-weekly psychotherapy before she was able to understand that the needs she tried to rise above throughout childhood and adolescence had finally crashed through the defenses she had built and were now demanding her attention.

Part of what Marcia had to come to terms with was that being bipolar wasn't easy. It wasn't just a matter of superficially accepting the diagnosis and moving on with her life. Through therapy she had to uncover the painful reality of what it meant for her to be bipolar and to grow up with a mother who was anything but stable.

Marcia had to recognize that she had learned to take care of her mother at a very early age, and in doing so had to prematurely give up any hope of having her own needs fulfilled by a loving and emotionally present mother. Instead, she learned to become her own parent, and as a result she readily moved toward a profession where taking care of others was central to the work. Throughout much of her life Marcia had been trying to make up for the unmet needs of a little girl with a bipolar mother. Once this recognition collided with her own bipolar reality, the accompanying psychotherapy became as important and as powerful as some of the cutting-edge medications that had been prescribed for her.

You see, bipolar disorder isn't just a set of symptoms. The symptoms very much play out in relation to who you are. No one's life is perfect and we all have our "stuff." In fact who you are, your personality, is very much a reflection of the important relationships of your childhood. When those relationships are loving and healthy, then you end up being pretty well put together. But when your childhood years are difficult and relationships with parents, siblings, or other key people in your life have been rough, then your resulting personality can be troubled. And when at the same time, you're genetically vulnerable to bipolar symptoms, then you've got a double whammy!

It's important to recognize that there is no blame intended here toward anyone. If you find that you're still struggling with unresolved childhood issues, it's truly not your fault. You didn't design the drama of your life; you came into the world as an infant without any choice. Nor is it the fault of other important people in your life. It may sometimes seem that it's their fault, but in most instances they were simply being themselves and trying their best to adapt, even if their efforts only made things harder. In other words, our personal dramas don't have villains; they usually just have people struggling with their own stuff. And this drama—the set, the lighting, the script, the props, and the other players—very much shapes who you are today. Even though you may sometimes feel like exiting stage right and leaving your past behind, you can't. You can only learn to deal with it and proceed forward. Some people do this more easily, and some still feel stuck in the drama.

If you gloss over this complexity, or if you superficially treat it as if it's just a set of chemical imbalances, then you're being set up for a fall—maybe not now, but sometime in the not too distant future. Nothing about this disorder is simple, but if that's the way it's being treated, or if that's the way you experience it, then quite possibly some important issues are being minimized or overlooked, and this won't serve you. The bottom line is that you've got to look deeply beneath the surface, because that's where you'll find some of the issues you need to explore in understanding your life with bipolar disorder.

writing your own story

Do you see yourself in any of the preceding sections? Do you identify with Ashley, Jason, or Marcia—or possibly even with the stories in chapter 1? Are you looking beneath your own surface?

One way you can reflect on your bipolar experience is to write a story about yourself. Tell your own story, from the point where you first began to experience any emotional ups and downs to the present. We're talking about your life circumstances, your interactions with significant others, your thoughts, feelings, and any mood instability—essentially, how your life has unfolded since you began to be aware of any bipolar symptoms. There's no specific form the story should take, and it can be as long or as short as you like. After all, it's all yours, just for your own eyes.

Once you've completed your story, try to step back from it and give it a read with as much objectivity as you can. Then ask yourself the following questions:

- What parts of your story stand out, and why?

- Is there anything in your story that resonates with the material in this chapter or in chapter 1?

- Does the story portray you as having any issues of denial or resistance?

- What have you learned about you as a result of writing your story?

If you can devote enough time to your writing to create a fairly in-depth narrative, chances are you'll find the effort will pay off. It isn't often that we stop and truly reflect on what we're going through. We hope you'll take the opportunity to do so and see what you learn.

finding acceptance

You've heard many references in this chapter to issues of vulnerability, fitting in, denial, anger, helplessness, and even pseudo-acceptance. What ties all of these together is the need to truly accept what you're going through.

Take stock of your life and then get on with it—it all sounds obvious. The difficulty with acceptance is the difference between what your life is and what you want it to be. That difference is often no small thing.

The Desire to Be Different

Just think of the time many of us spend in fantasy. Often our fantasies reflect our wishes. Fantasies of falling in love can make us feel a little less lonely. Or if you're in a relationship, then you might have fantasies of a better relationship—being with someone who is more attractive, more loving, or more responsible. "If only he or she were different, then I'd feel better." Or perhaps you have fantasies of a job that has more glamour or status, or one that pays a higher salary. Sometimes fantasies can revolve around being thinner, stronger, taller, or having larger breasts, smaller breasts, more hair, better health—you name it. Just take a moment to conjure up your wish list. Most of us can easily generate an "if only" list without much effort.

Much time and energy can go toward wanting to be different, and sometimes this focus shows healthy desire for change. Of course we want to be better in every way we can. This is good! Otherwise, what would be the point of our New Year's resolutions?

But with bipolar disorder, you may see ways that you want to be different because you don't like the way the illness affects who you are, yet you're unable to change them. That's the painful part. There are many aspects of our existence that aren't changeable. If we could more readily embrace that notion and accept our uniqueness as part of our identity, life would be much easier. But we face one big obstacle: truly accepting the painful losses when things never heal or recover.

Avoiding the Pain of Loss

Let's say you experienced a childhood where your parents were unhappy in their marriage, and they divorced when you were seven or eight years old. Additionally, let's assume their conflicts and emotionally abusive arguing was present in your family as far back as you can remember. Truly accepting that profound influence on your development means letting go of the hope that those painful memories will someday be gone or, better yet, healed, or that you will someday have a loving, intact family—or even that you could have had the kind of childhood that other kids seemed to have.

Unfortunately, if you're amongst those who grew up in an unstable and disrupted family environment, the painful experiences did happen and those memories are stored in your brain. And if you're not a child of divorced parents, then simply let yourself think about anything else within your history that was emotionally painful and unwanted. It did happen and you can't change it.

Now, because the memories are painful, you may avoid thinking about them. That's a normal way of trying to cope with a painful experience. In fact, many people may think they would be better off if they could just find a way of shutting out or distancing themselves from their own painful feelings, negative thoughts, or memories that create difficulties for them. If there were methods out there that were truly effective, then it would make sense to try to learn them. But there's one very substantial problem with this way of coping. There isn't any kind of mental lobotomy where we can disconnect from emotionally painful thoughts or feelings without being vulnerable to those same thoughts or feelings coming back to haunt us sooner or later.

Many people try this kind of emotional distancing, and if you're one of them you may even find that your efforts are partially effective. But if and when those unwanted mental experiences make themselves known again, especially if they emerge rather suddenly, you're more likely to feel overwhelmed by their intensity if you haven't learned the smart way to manage those feelings. Simply put, avoiding a painful reality doesn't help you to learn how to deal with it. Your defenses buy you time away from the discomfort, which is good. But the outcome doesn't help you to become better at managing the discomfort, which is not good.

Grieving Your Losses and Letting Them Go

So how do we face those parts of ourselves that we don't want to face? Or more to the point, how do you find some comfort and acceptance with all of the losses associated with bipolar disorder? Some people can find comfort and acceptance on their own. Others may need professional help.

How do you know what's best for you? The answer probably has to do with how successfully you find you are managing the transition into being bipolar or learning that you have bipolar disorder. If you find that after many months you're still struggling with feelings of anger, shame, grief, and strong desires to deny or reject the diagnosis, then it's probably time to look for professional help, typically in the form of psychotherapy.

And what's the task or the goal of the therapy? It's really a combination of acceptance and developing the skills to manage your life effectively. But initially, the key to facing your bipolar disorder involves the development of your capacity to accept the changes that you will need to make to live with it; that means allowing yourself room for any accompanying emotional pain, without denial or resistance. You need to explore your reactions to the diagnosis and encounter whatever thoughts and emotions you may find. You need to become a frequent traveler in the realm of your own bipolar experience so that you can get to know the bipolar landscape.

Let's look at an analogy, more within the physical realm. Imagine you have a knee injury with fairly chronic implications. Rather than doing everything within your power to try to run, imagine accepting that running or other activities requiring strong legs just aren't in the cards and that sometimes you've got to sit on the sidelines and watch others run, skateboard, or whatever. And further, imagine that each time you recognize that you can't do what you really want to do, you also let yourself feel some grief over the loss of your capacity—not fun, but more adaptive than trying to achieve the impossible.

After having visited this loss many times, imagine that something occurs in life that again reminds you of this limitation. Rather than feeling overwhelmed, you go, "Oh yeah, I know what these feelings are. They're no surprise. I don't like them, but I can accept them." And with the exception of a few moments, you don't skip a beat because you've learned how to live with the painful feelings. And now you don't struggle against the experience. You don't push it away. You don't try to deny it. You let it in, and you let yourself think about it. You also allow for your feelings of disappointment and loss, which may never quite go away, and then you move on to what's next. Truly, this is a whole lot easier than trying to run when you can't and only ending up in more pain.

The process we're referring to is no different when you're dealing with some of the limitations imposed by bipolar disorder. It's a matter of accepting that which you can't change and mourning the "you" that you once hoped you would become.

The feelings of loss and limitation that we're referring to aren't pretty—there's a lot of anger and sadness wrapped up in these feelings. But the more you're able to simply let them happen, the less likely you will be to get caught up in maladaptive defenses.

So the next obvious question is, how do you learn to let these feelings happen without becoming overwhelmed by all the complex issues? Unfortunately, there isn't an easy answer. But one thing's for sure: ignoring your disorder isn't the answer. For most, the consistent support from friends, family, and loved ones is absolutely essential. On top of that, there are multiple routes toward emotional and psychological health, including choices such as medication, psychotherapy, mindfulness, meditation, and many more. Each of you must find the combination of approaches that works best for you.

We're not inviting you to a party. We are inviting you to face the very real complications and losses that may be involved in your experience with bipolar disorder. Occasionally your hypomania may interfere with your work productivity. Sometimes a manic episode may knock you out of commission for several weeks. Sometimes your depression will pull you down. And sometimes your need for a full night's sleep may interfere with the spontaneity of a night out with friends. These are all real possibilities. The adaptations you'll need to make to minimize these derailments will depend upon the unique shape and patterns of your life.

You will have to modify your lifestyle to appropriately adapt and manage your intermittent bipolar symptoms; that's real. And the more you can develop true inner self-acceptance, the more likely you will be to find fulfillment in many different aspects of your life. You don't have to be the picture of perfect mental health in order to be loved. But you do have to accept your limitations in order to be whole.

CHAPTER FOUR

what you can do: the four S's of bipolar stability

There's a lot you can do on your own to maintain good mental health. In fact, your stability depends a lot on your actions and choices.

At the end of chapter 1 we compared living with bipolar to being carried down a river on a raft. The good news is that you have a set of oars on board. Whether your trip down the river is manageable or not depends on the direction and control that you bring to the experience. In other words, you don't have to be a passive passenger being swept down the bipolar river. In this chapter we'll provide you with the four keys to staying stable when you have bipolar disorder. We refer to these as the four S's of bipolar stability:

- Creating a *structured* life.

- Managing your *stress*.

- Getting good *sleep*.

- Learning to *self-monitor*.

creating a structured life

As you know, stress can aggravate your bipolar symptoms. While life can be turbulent and unpredictable at times, it's important to create a daily rhythm that is relatively steady and predictable. None of us have full control over what unfolds in the future; we all hit rough spots from time to time, no matter how much we try to control our circumstances. Still, it's important, especially when you're living with bipolar disorder, to try to create a steady routine in order to lessen the impact of the inevitable heavy weather that you'll encounter along the way.

Let's imagine that your normal way of dealing is to wing it, to fly by the seat of your pants. You wake up each day and you see where life takes you. Maybe you go to school or work; maybe you don't. You let your impulses and desires guide you. If it feels good or if it's interesting, you go for it. And then you see where those choices take you. Each day is new and potentially exciting, or perhaps even disruptive, depending upon what you get into. And as for planning, it's not in your vocabulary—you get the picture.

Now imagine a completely different life, where your schedule and your commitments for the near future are laid out ahead of time. You wake up at 7:30 on Mondays, Wednesdays, and Fridays because you have classes between 9:00 and 12:00. You also get yourself to a quiet place to study between 2:00 and 4:00 on each of those days...well, maybe not on Friday. And for those of you in the 8:00 to 5:00 workweek, you know the drill. In addition, you keep the activities of your days laid out on a weekly schedule so that most of the time you know what's coming next because you've planned it. You've even done the same with your work assignments. No last-minute frantic cramming or completing work projects! You're even relaxed because you have things completed ahead of schedule. Sound dull? Maybe. But it will keep stress at bay, and you'll find that you're feeling more on top of things.

People with bipolar disorder do much better over time when they integrate a moderate degree of structure into their lives—and when they work at developing the discipline to stick to that structure. This is true for two different reasons.

First, for people who are bipolar, it doesn't take much to activate intense emotions. A poignant movie might easily bring you to tears, an upbeat song may have you feeling joyful, or a disappointing outcome might cause you to plunge into self-doubt. If you live that life, you'll find that this brings an emotional intensity that you might not otherwise have if you weren't bipolar. But at the same time, you may find that you repeatedly feel you're not very effective in keeping on a steady course. Essentially, the current is stronger than your paddling and you're being tossed about with little control. A structured life can help you keep on course.

Second, people with bipolar disorder are usually more impulsive when they're feeling up or, conversely, shut down when they're feeling blue. Quite literally, the regions of your brain responsible for mood and emotions exert more influence than regions involving judgment and planning (Nesse and Williams 1994). But that doesn't mean you have no control over your life and moods. If you learn to embrace structure (scheduling, planning, and organization), you'll find that you're less impulsive and less inclined to give in to a depressive funk. With enough practice, you'll find that this structure in your life will help keep your mood and emotions from running your life. Remember, hypomania or depression can take you into dangerous waters. Once you begin to develop momentum in either direction, no matter how hard you paddle it can be harder to slow it down.

recommendations for creating helpful structure

1. Get an appointment book or personal electronic organizer, and use it.

2. Create a weekly schedule of commitments, including those to yourself.

3. Create a list of short-term and long-term school- or work-related goals.

4. Create plans to accompany these goals. How are you going to get them done and within what time frame?

5. Wake up and go to sleep within a half hour of the same time each day, even on weekends!

6. Commit to regular exercise at least three times a week on a consistent schedule.

7. Plan to eat your meals around the same time each day.

8. Take your medications on a regular schedule. You can find a pill box at your local drugstore that can help to organize your medicine.

The Challenges of Creating Structure

If you're somewhere between late high school and the point where you've completed your education, you may think that all of this talk of structure is way over the top. After all, you're in the stage of your life where you finally have more freedom than you've ever had before, and what a relief, after being told what to do and when to do it for most of your life! It only makes sense that you want to take advantage of that freedom.

Okay, so here's where it's important to stop and recognize that you've got a disorder that requires special handling. You still have your independence. You are free to handle your disorder your way, under your control. You'll face choices like those faced by others your age, but you'll have to learn to make these choices based on the question, Will it be good for me? rather than, Will it feel good? That's a very different question. As you build healthy structure into your life, you'll find the benefits outweigh the pleasures of being impulsive.

While you may have moments where you'll want to throw caution to the wind—and other times when you actually do—over time you will come to see that establishing structure will be one of the more important tasks to master.

managing stress

It would be nice if a structured and disciplined life could protect you against stress. Unfortunately, it doesn't. It just lessens the likelihood that the stress will be too much for you. No matter what, life during your late teens and twenties is a very stressful time.

Consider the many stresses that you might face during these years: academics, balancing academics with other involvements, establishing new relationships, getting into one of your top-choice colleges, living away from home for the first time, selecting an appropriate major or career, managing differences with roommates, having enough money, facing the challenges of a first job, becoming financially self-sufficient, the ups and downs of love relationships, and so on.

Everyone who transitions from adolescence to adulthood faces these stresses. If you're lucky, you get through it all in one piece and learn a lot in the process. In fact, experiences of moderate stress that result in learning and mastery are important for us. They strengthen us for future challenging situations, which, in the long run, promotes stable and healthy functioning. But while everyone experiences stress, most don't have bipolar disorder. So stress management is particularly important for you.

Even with good stress management, you're likely to encounter problems when high stress levels are frequent and sustained. Occasionally, very high stress occurs because of disruptive events that you can't control, such as when a friend or family member dies or you go through a painful breakup. Sometimes bad stuff happens. But even when bad stuff happens, how we respond makes the difference between a negative outcome and a positive one. Stress itself isn't so much the problem; it's how we respond to it.

If you're under repeated stress and don't manage it well, then instead of feeling a sense of mastery, you'll only feel more stressed-out. If you keep producing high levels of stress-related hormones and neurochemicals, your body's natural capacity to regulate its own stress response breaks down. You feel like you can't relax or slow down. You can't sleep well because you're always worrying. You can't just chill even when you try.

Okay, you get it. Continued stress feels bad. But what's the big deal?

The big deal is this: *If you're genetically vulnerable to developing bipolar disorder, prolonged stress can actually cause the onset of bipolar symptoms and increase your chances of relapse once you've developed the disorder.* So if you've got depression, anxiety, bipolar disorder, or some other mental or emotional disorder in your family's history, or if you've already been diagnosed with a mood disorder, stress is definitely not your friend. In fact, stress can be more like the unexpected ten-foot waterfall as you round the bend of the river.

Let's imagine a really rough couple of weeks where you're irritable, physically tense, and generally stressed. Your body can't relax and your thinking is accelerated because your mind is working overtime trying to find solutions. You can't find the switch to turn it all off, so you're also struggling with insomnia, which is making your body and mind even less resilient. Or let's consider a different picture, where things aren't going your way and, instead of growing anxious, you're slipping into a funk. Your self-esteem is hitting bottom, you're withdrawing from the world, and you're feeling like you want to give up. And if you don't start feeling better, you might even try using alcohol, pot, sleeping pills, amphetamines, or worse to bring about some relief—unhealthy coping strategies that bring their own sets of problems. This all leads to a downward spiral: sustained stress → feeling miserable → erosion of physical and mental resilience → diminished judgment and unclear thinking → maladaptive behavior → creation of more stressful situations → feeling more miserable. You can see where this leads. Stress will capsize your raft like a set of class 5 rapids.

So what do you do instead? You become a certified river rafting guide! We're only half kidding. You quite literally need to commit yourself to developing effective stress management techniques and to really work at becoming good at them. As you'll see in the next section, sleep is also a big deal for the bipolar person. Therefore it's important to practice your stress management techniques at night before you go to sleep. We're talking about practices such as deep breathing exercises, progressive muscle relaxation, yoga, meditation, and more. There is much to learn about stress management, and you will develop your own preferences that work for you. To give you a start, we've provided one breathing and relaxation exercise, adapted from *The Relaxation and Stress Reduction Workbook* (Davis, Robbins, and McKay 2008).

breathing for tension release and increased awareness

1. If you're in a place where you can lie down, do so. If not, remain seated but try to get as comfortable and relaxed as you can.

2. Slowly breathe in through your nose. Breathe deeply into the lower part of your abdomen (expanding your diaphragm—the big muscle below your rib cage—downward to expand your lungs) as you say to yourself, "Breathe in."

3. Hold your breath for a moment before you exhale.

4. Exhale slowly and deeply as you say to yourself, "Relax."

5. Pause and wait for your next natural breath.

6. As you inhale slowly and then hold your breath for a moment, notice the parts of your body that tense up.

7. As you exhale, feel the tension naturally leaving your body. With each exhalation, you will feel more and more relaxed, as you let go of more and more tension.

8. When the thoughts, feelings, and sensations catch your attention, just notice them and return to your breathing.

9. Practice for five to twenty minutes at a time.

10. Once you've mastered this exercise, practice using it several times a day in neutral situations; that is, in nonstressful situations. Finally, start using it in stressful situations to reduce your tension. Simply take several diaphragmatic breaths, say the words "breathe in" and "relax," and let go of the tension on the exhalation.

11. Now focus on your sensations of relaxation.

You can find different exercises and approaches to explore by referring to appendix A, Internet Resources, in the back of this book. Keep in mind, we're not asking you to become a stress management guru within the next month. What we are saying is that your success with stress management will be important in effectively managing your bipolar disorder. Just learning one or two key stress management techniques can make a world of difference in your ability to manage the ups and downs of life.

getting good sleep

Sleep. Think about it for a moment. It's something that most of us do every night. Granted, it may feel more like it's something that happens to us. We get into bed, close our eyes, and if everything works as it should, then we gently drift into sleep. Our conscious awareness truly takes a rest while different cycles of brain activity continue throughout the night. We then wake up seven or eight hours later and return to consciousness. Unless we work nights, we generally get sleepy a few hours after dark and gradually wake up with the arrival of the morning light.

Realistically speaking, the sleep cycle isn't always this normal, smooth, and regular for everyone; however, the fundamentals of this recurring sleep and wake cycle reflect important aspects of what we refer to as *circadian rhythms*. These are the body's recurrent rhythms of alertness, energy, activity, fatigue, and sleep corresponding to the twenty-four hours of the earth's daily rotation.

For most people who are not bipolar, these rhythms remain fairly constant. But if you're bipolar, when you're under stress these rhythms easily go awry. If you're depressed, you may find that it's difficult to wake up in the morning. You may also find yourself going back to sleep at different times during the day. Without the "on" switch of energy and alertness, your body is lacking what it needs to move forward.

In episodes of hypomania and mania, just the opposite occurs. Your heightened energy doesn't naturally slow down toward the end of the day. Your acceleration remains on and the natural cues of nighttime darkness don't prompt the drowsiness that then progresses toward sleep. Even when exhaustion finally does take you into sleep, you may find you awaken only a few hours later with your accelerator still pressed to the floor. What makes this worse is that you can't seem to find the switch to turn it all off.

The point is that too much or too little sleep can have a profound impact on mood and energy, especially if you're bipolar. Sleep deprivation, particularly when sustained, can and often does bring on hypomania or mania. Essentially, all it takes is one night of less than adequate sleep to trigger a hypomanic episode. If you only get two or three hours' sleep on Saturday and Sunday night, the following day will potentially be your manic Monday. Two or three consecutive nights of not enough sleep can be like throwing a lit match on a large pile of dry kindling. Once lit, your elevated mood and energy will make you more inclined to resist sleep, adding additional fuel to the fire. On the other hand, if you sleep too much it can pave the way for a depressive episode.

Adequate sleep (approximately eight hours per night) and a nightly sleep schedule where you go to sleep and get up at relatively consistent times are imperative for the stability of a bipolar person. We can't overstate this point.

You're probably beginning to see some themes here: application of daily structure, effective stress management, and consistent sleep habits. It's probably self-evident how these would help you be more stable. The problem is that just as we pointed out in our discussion of structure, these lifestyle practices tend to clash completely with the typical lifestyle of someone your age.

Think of being out with friends on a weekend where your activities don't really get rolling until 10 p.m.—and there you are feeling your own internal pressure to return home and be asleep by midnight. Or you're on a date and the connection feels right, but it's already 11 p.m. and you don't feel ready to end the evening. And then there are the continuous requirements of academics. You've got a fifteen-page paper due tomorrow and you know you're going to need most of the night to finish writing it. Or you're deep in a group project and the group plans to work through the night. If you're dealing with the rigors of a full-time job, you may find that by Friday evening you're exhausted from a hard week at work. You just want to sleep in on Saturday morning for as long as you can. The thought of awakening by 8 or 9 a.m. in order to stick to your sleep schedule feels almost impossible. What do you do with all of this?

You'll have to start making choices that are different from the choices of most others you know. You won't do it because you like it. You'll make your choices because you know they're healthy ones. Most people with type 1 diabetes don't enjoy injecting themselves with insulin and going without desserts, but they do these things because the consequence of not doing them is much worse. If you knew that you would lose consciousness and lapse into a coma without consistent sleep, you'd probably make sure that you kept to a consistent sleep schedule.

What makes this all much more complicated is that managing your bipolar disorder is going to affect your social life. It's one thing to pass up the slice of birthday cake or to excuse yourself in order to give yourself an insulin injection. It's quite another thing to have to say good-bye to your friends and return home because you need your sleep. We'll explore this difference in more depth in the next chapter. For now, it's important to recognize that if you want to successfully live with bipolar disorder, there are things you can do to enhance your ability to remain stable. Establishing a regular sleep schedule in the midst of an irregular phase of life is a big challenge. But it is doable.

---

sleep checklist

- Get eight hours of sleep each night.

- Go to sleep and get up at the same time with consistency, even on weekends.

- Don't nap during the day, even if you're sleepy.

- Tell others about your need to manage your sleep in order to stay healthy.

---

learning to self-monitor

Let's return to our discussion of your raft, but shift the image a little and imagine you're in a kayak. One of the things that's important when kayaking is finding your vertical center. In other words, you want to remain upright. If you feel a slight tilting to your right or left, you make subtle movements to counteract the tilt. Maybe you lean your head or torso a little bit to one side. Maybe you shift the position of your paddle. Essentially, you're listening to your body's cues about balance and you're making appropriate adjustments. Successfully managing bipolar is not that different. The big challenge, however, is being able to observe your own processes with clarity.

The Difficulties of Seeing Yourself Clearly

When you're kayaking, you usually don't want to tip over, unless you're rolling for the fun of it. Most of the time, the goal is to stay upright. In fact, the thought of capsizing is usually uncomfortable. When you're bipolar, the thought of a significant mood and energy shift may also be uncomfortable, but unless you're very tuned in to your own variability, it's not easy to recognize the changes when they are happening.

Feeling these changes is especially hard with hypomania, which usually arrives with good feelings: increased energy, faster thinking, increased creativity, and feelings of pleasure. It's not like there's anything going on that tells you that you're about to tip. In fact, if you've been feeling down for a while, the arrival of hypomania can feel like a great relief. But now you're faced with quite the dilemma: the very changes that make you feel good could potentially be bad for you, but you don't realize the danger because you feel good!

Experiencing depression is quite different. You usually know when you're feeling down, and you're also aware that it feels bad. However, the low energy and apathy that often come with depression can be challenging to your efforts to self-correct a downward slide. Imagine one morning you wake up feeling really low. You know it, but because you're feeling low, you don't care to do anything about it. Instead of getting out of bed or exercising or going to work, you just let it all slide. And by late afternoon you find you're in a whopping depression. By the time you're fully acknowledging that you've slid into a depressive funk, you may no longer have the energy or resilience to try to climb out.

These very challenges bring us to a new variation in the kinds of changes to your lifestyle and attitude that will contribute to your mental health. You'll need to develop your own fine-tuned self-observation skills so you become mindful of your ongoing variations in mood, thought, and energy. You'll have to learn the difference between what's normal for you and what's a sign of a potentially dangerous shift in mood.

Developing Mindfulness

To give you feel for what we're talking about, let's take a few moments to try out a brief self-awareness exercise.

---

1. Let yourself reflect inward. Simply ask, What am I experiencing right now?

2. What are your physical sensations? Can you feel your breath being drawn in and out? Do you feel your body pressing against any external surfaces, such as a chair, a bed, or a desk? What parts of your body are you more consciously aware of? Do you note any tensions? Where are they in your body? Are you comfortable or uncomfortable in your body?

3. Now let your awareness shift to your sense of physical energy. Is it adequate, low, shaky, or high? Do you feel awake and alert or possibly fatigued? Are you comfortable sitting still or not? If not, how would you like to move?

4. Now let yourself focus upon your surrounding physical space. As you become aware of your surroundings, what do you hear? Are there any new sounds you're aware of as you focus more sharply? What do you see surrounding the pages of this book? What else might you be aware of in your surrounding space?

5. Now let yourself reflect upon your thoughts or reactions in response to these questions. Do you experience anything surprising or unexpected? Do you want more questions? Do you want to stop?

What you've just done is sharpen your attention to your present experience by reflecting upon that experience. You've allowed yourself to observe what's happening in the moment instead of simply being carried along with it. We all do this—sometimes more, sometimes less, depending on how we feel and depending on the situation. Of course, observing yourself is much more easy and pleasant if you're sitting quietly on a hillside watching the sunset than it is when you're caught in bumper-to-bumper rush-hour traffic. But that doesn't mean it's impossible in rush-hour traffic. You would just need to make a more conscious effort to disconnect from the stresses of traffic and simply observe your experience.

For the bipolar person, this kind of self-awareness or mindfulness is crucial to maintaining healthy balance. You see, unlike the diabetic, you don't have the luxury of being able to use a tiny drop of blood to test your bipolar emotional balance. For the most part, you've got to rely on your own capacity to monitor and assess your different mood states. We're not suggesting that you constantly remain on guard, vigilant, and prepared to shut down any subtle shift in mood, thought, or energy. After all, some changes in our emotions and levels of energy are perfectly appropriate and healthy. Plus, it would be a drag to feel the same all the time. But what we are suggesting is that you become highly attuned to your own baseline of mood, thinking, and energy. You want to become very familiar with what is typical and usual for you.

As you become more knowledgeable and familiar with your baseline, you'll learn to maintain a subtle, observing detachment that can calmly note any changes or variations in your experience. You'll want to simply monitor the flow of your own experience while staying connected to your center, the energetic and emotional equivalent of your vertical midline. When things begin to shift in either direction, you mentally take note of the change. If you judge the change to be appropriate based on what's going on around you, then you simply let it happen. If your mind speeds up, you feel a lot of physical energy, and you're tempted to take impulsive actions, then your observing awareness should also begin to warn you that you need to be cautious. The same would hold true with a shift in the direction of depression. It's like you're learning how to become your own lifeguard. The more practiced you become with this style of mindfulness, the more natural and effective it will begin to feel.

In recent years the concept of mindfulness has drawn much attention, and just as we advised in our discussion of stress management, there is a wide range of information readily available to you online. (See appendix A, Internet Resources, for specific mindfulness resources.)

Developing a Sleep, Mood, and Energy Chart

As we've pointed out, self-awareness can have its limitations when your ability to perceive yourself is directly affected by mood changes. It is therefore important for you to gather and keep a record of objective external information, such as the Sleep, Mood, and Energy Chart that we'll present in this section.

We've already discussed how sleep can have direct impact on your mood and energy. You'll also recall that a change in the amount you sleep can be one of the first signs of an emerging shift in your mood. When your sleep cycle begins to shift toward longer or shorter sleep, changes in mood and energy will often follow within one to two days. Monitoring your sleep, mood, and energy will provide you important ongoing information about your overall mood stability. To help you track trends and changes in these three variables, we've developed a chart aptly named the Sleep, Mood, and Energy Chart. Instructions for its use and a blank chart are provided in appendix B.

We all can expect some variability in sleep, mood, and energy, usually over one or two days' time. If you're up late studying for an important test or finishing a project for work, then you may feel tired the next day. If you're going through a breakup you may feel down while also having trouble sleeping. Again, this is normal life stuff. That's not what you're watching out for. You use the Sleep, Mood, and Energy Chart to look for changes that appear to be unusually sharp, or changes that show clear trends over time.

Remember that with bipolar disorder, there is typically an inverse relationship between sleep and the other two variables of energy and mood. So when you sleep less because of a hypomanic shift, your mood and energy typically increase. Similarly, when your sleep extends beyond what is normal for you, then your mood and energy decline as a function of depression.

On the following page we've provided an example of a completed chart for a person who is experiencing the first week of a hypomanic episode. You'll note a clear inverse trend: as the number of hours of sleep decreases over several days, mood and energy rise. It looks as if this person might be headed toward a full manic episode, though realistically speaking you will rarely get to see a completed chart on someone with full mania. During a typical manic episode, day-to-day functioning (including chart keeping) usually unravels.

If the person in the hypomanic chart example happened to be you, here are some examples of actions that you might need to take:

- Calling or meeting with your mental health professional and speaking with him or her about what to do next.

- Talking with your mental health care providers about having your lithium blood level checked.

- Talking with your doctor about increasing or changing the doses of your mood stabilizing medications.

- Talking with your doctors about additional strategies and medication to help you get to sleep.

- Returning to live with your primary support system (parents, other relatives, close friends, or others who have your back).

You can see how the ability to track important changes in your day-to-day experience might encourage you to take necessary preventative actions. We recommend that you consider using the chart over at least two to three months. It will take that long before you can see whether the overview that it provides is helpful. There are also many other charts currently available to people with bipolar disorder. Each is unique and helpful in its own right and may be accessed online by searching the Internet for "bipolar mood chart."

Sleep, Mood, and Energy Chart

Sleep, Mood and Energy		Dates: _____ through _____						
		M	T	W	Th	F	Sa	S
Hours of Sleep	12+							
	9–11							
	7–8	X						
	5–6		X	X				
	3–4				X	X	X	
	0–2							X
Mood	High						X	X
	Mildly ↑				X	X		
	Midrange		X	X				
	Mildly ↓	X						
	Depressed							
Energy Level	High						X	X
	Mildly ↑				X	X		
	Midrange		X	X				
	Mildly ↓	X						
	Depressed							

Additional Reminders to Yourself

If you've had bipolar for a few years and have experienced a few bipolar episodes, you probably already have crisis preparedness plans in place, just as you would if someone in your family were epileptic. You would have learned how to care for your loved one during a seizure and you'd have phone numbers readily available for the neurologist and emergency transport to the hospital. As soon as you recognized that a seizure was occurring you'd kick into gear with your emergency response plan.

Preparing for bipolar instability is like emergency preparedness for epilepsy, except that to recognize the onset of instability, you need to depend on your ability to see yourself accurately. An epileptic seizure is usually identifiable, but hypomania may be harder to spot because of the effects it has upon your thoughts and feelings. So in addition to adequate structure, stress management skills, good sleep, and well-developed self-monitoring techniques, it can also be helpful to create clear and concise written reminders to yourself that outline what happens to you during a hypomanic episode. We refer to this as a Symptom Reminder List. In addition to these reminders, it's advisable to have a clear set of written instructions about helpful actions to take in response to your hypomania.

Creating a Symptom Reminder List

The first step is to take some time to put together your Symptom Reminder List. Now let's assume you've got some other people in your life (such as a lover, a roommate, friends, or parents) who have been around during your previous hypomanic changes. If so, you should speak with them and ask them to share their observations with you about your previous hypomanic behaviors. You then take this new information, add it to your own, and make a list of the behavioral changes that you typically undergo when you shift from normal or midrange mood into hypomania. You should pay particular attention to the early warning signs of your hypomanic behavioral changes. By noticing these and catching them early, you may increase the odds that you can make appropriate and necessary adjustments early enough to head off the arrival of hypomania or to keep it from developing into full mania or a mixed episode. You'll also have a source of external feedback that may help you to break through some of the denial and poor judgment common to the hypomanic experience, such as thinking, "I don't need to take my medicine anymore because I feel great." Here is an example of what a completed Symptom Reminder List might look like.

When I first begin to feel hypomanic...

1. I feel unusually alert.

2. I feel optimistic and enthused, even about things that would normally be boring.

3. Talking with others is easier for me.

4. I don't feel fatigued during the day and I can get by with two or three hours less sleep.

5. I don't want to study because there are many more things I'd rather be doing.

When my hypomania becomes stronger and progresses beyond a few days...

1. My need for sleep declines further. Maybe I only need three or four hours total each night.

2. My energy feels big.

3. My thoughts are moving very fast. Sometimes it becomes difficult to hold on to a thought.

4. I feel sexy.

5. I become flirtatious.

6. I want to go shopping. When I do, I spend more than I should.

7. I find that I love to cook (usually I don't).

8. Sometimes I'll try to cook two or three meals at the same time. My kitchen becomes pretty messy.

9. I feel like I want to stop taking my medication.

When you have completed your Symptom Reminder List, set it aside somewhere handy, where you'll see it and remember to refer to it when you suspect the onset of hypomania. The next time you have the sense that your mood is becoming unstable, your list will be available for your reference. The list will allow you to compare your experience with descriptions you've already created. If there is a high degree of overlap between the two, then you might reasonably conclude that a hypomanic episode is brewing.

Occasionally, someone who knows you well may express concern about some of your recent behaviors, noting you're becoming hypomanic. Perhaps you haven't yet felt or noticed anything different, and you may feel like dismissing or disagreeing with those observations. But before writing them off, you'd be wise to pause and check your Symptom Reminder List. You may find that the very things this person noticed were things that you had listed as your hypomanic symptoms. In other words, your hypomania was getting in the way of your accurate self-perception. Once you're clear about the presence of a hypomanic influence, then you can begin to take appropriate corrective steps.

Creating a Healthy Actions List

After creating your Symptom Reminder List, your next step is to identify what actions are typically healthy and corrective in response to your hypomanic experience. We'll refer to this as your Healthy Actions List. It is very helpful to have this list available to remind you of the various things you can do to stabilize your mood.

The following Healthy Actions List is an example that stems from the preceding Symptom Reminder List.

Things I can do to help myself when I'm hypomanic:

1. Call my psychiatrist.

2. Tell her what's happening on the phone and get her initial recommendations.

3. Make an appointment to see her ASAP.

4. Follow her recommendations about medication changes, even if I'm reluctant to do so.

5. Don't drink any caffeine after about 11 a.m.

6. Before going to bed at night, take a hot bath or shower to relax.

7. After a bath or shower, do the relaxation exercises I've learned.

8. Follow sleep hygiene rules. Go to bed at the same time every night, even if I don't feel tired. Read or do something else that isn't exciting until I'm eventually able to fall asleep.

9. Don't go out in the evening after about 10.

10. Give my credit card to someone I trust.

11. Don't hook up with anyone sexually until I'm back to feeling stable, and I'm certain that I still want to.

12. Stick with my normal daily schedule.

13. Don't skip any classes.

14. If I'm having difficulty doing schoolwork, get a note from my psychiatrist and speak with my teachers about what's going on.

15. Only cook one meal at a time.

16. Let my roommate know what's happening and ask her to tell me if she thinks I may be doing anything that's unhealthy or outrageous.

17. Don't drink alcohol.

18. Don't smoke pot.

So far, we've been focusing on reminders to self for dealing with hypomania. You can use the same process to deal with an episode of depression, though obviously the content of your Symptom Reminder List and the corresponding Healthy Actions List would be different. But the same principles apply: reaching out for help and attempting to take healthy and corrective actions. One additional piece of advice: Keep these lists in a location where you can easily find them when you need them, or just go ahead and post them on the refrigerator or the bathroom mirror. It's hard enough to remember important details when your thoughts are flying at warp speed. You don't want to add another layer of complexity by hiding important information from yourself!

You have less control over your disorder than you would like and more influence than you can imagine. A few episodes of depression, hypomania, mania, or mixtures of these can make you feel helpless, with little control over your life. This perspective is a road to nowhere. Conversely, if you *create a structured life, manage your stress, get good sleep,* and *learn to self-monitor,* your efforts *will* reduce episodes and increase your sense of mastery over this illness.

CHAPTER FIVE

how open can you be about your disorder?

Some medical disorders are easier to disclose than others, and some disclose themselves. Bipolar disorder is often one of the self-disclosing ones. In other words, you won't always get to choose who knows; however, when you do choose to tell, remember there is no right or wrong decision. You will find your own comfort level with sharing this information.

transparency with others

Some of the recommended lifestyle changes we discussed in the previous chapter will tend to draw attention to your bipolar disorder. People who are more involved in your day-to-day life (roommates, lovers, or family, for example) will tend to notice your sleep schedule, your mood changes, or that you're taking medication. Additionally, there are times when you may not want your disorder to be hidden from others. It's a part of who you are, and those who come to know you well will recognize this. Besides, as you'll discover, when others know about your disorder they can join your helping network, which supports you with a reality check and a safety net when you shift into a period of mood instability. So it's actually important to have some people who know about your disorder. Full privacy about it probably won't serve you well.

Coming Out

The notion of "coming out" is an interesting one. We're accustomed to hearing it used in reference to a person's decision to disclose his or her sexual identity. Though bipolar has nothing to do with sexuality, coming out as a bipolar person poses similar issues. If you choose to come out, you'll likely receive all kinds of reactions, from some people telling you it makes little difference to them to some who will withdraw or even talk about you behind your back. The sad reality is that not many people are well educated about mental disorders, and you'll encounter some who have biases and misconceptions. So you'll want to make careful choices about whom you tell and whom you don't.

In chapter 2 we said that honesty about your disorder, in most cases, will serve you well. And while you'll find that's mostly true, there will also be times when the better strategy is to be discreet about whom you tell—at least until you get to know them well. Our best advice is to start slow and trust your gut. Remember, privacy is not dishonesty, and sometimes it's just good sense.

Acquaintances and Friends

Of your different relationships, acquaintances and friendships probably represent the largest numbers of the people in your life. These relationships represent connections that range from superficial interactions to your closest friendships, the ones where you share your innermost thoughts and feelings. Your choice to share the fact that you're bipolar will reflect the depth of your connection with others. Consider those acquaintances where you meet someone and say little more than "Hey, how's it going?" Certainly you wouldn't say, "Hey, how's it going? I'm bipolar!" But with people you're really close to, why wouldn't you share your bipolar reality?

Okay, there are some common answers to this rhetorical question. You don't want them to think you're crazy. You don't want them to think less of you or that you require special handling. But consider this: you'll worry less about their response once you actually see their response, and, likewise, their concern will be relieved and they'll have a chance to understand when they see you handle your bipolar issues. You don't want to have to pretend with your closest friends. That robs you and them of the openness and honesty that's part of friendship.

Imagine you have a close friend whom you think you know quite well. And then you discover that she's been keeping a whole dimension of her life hidden from you. You'd probably feel some degree of hurt and disappointment because of her keeping that secret. You'd probably think she never trusted you, and you'd probably wonder how much trust there ever had been in the relationship. You might even pull back some yourself. Even if she kept this important information from you in order to protect the friendship, it could possibly have just the opposite effect.

And now consider the question of whether you'd truly want to establish close relationships with people who couldn't handle the fact that you're bipolar. Probably not. You want relationships with those who can truly get to know you, understand you, enjoy you, and possibly even step up to help if you ever need it.

It'll be easy to decide not to tell people who don't know you very well about your bipolar disorder. And with people who have known and been close to you for a long time, it will be straightforward to decide to tell them. The tricky part happens with people you know beyond a superficial level but with whom you haven't yet established a strong connection. Here is where you'll find the greatest uncertainty about how to proceed in coming out. Let's look at a few examples. As you read them, try to place yourself in the person's shoes and then think about how you would respond.

→ **Elizabeth**

Twenty-year-old Elizabeth works full-time as a food server in a busy, upscale restaurant. She's had her bipolar diagnosis for three years now and her current functioning is pretty stable. When she works the evening shift, customers are no longer seated after midnight, though she's usually serving and cleaning up until about 2 a.m. There's an all-night restaurant and bar nearby, and often several of her coworkers hang out there after work for a few hours. Elizabeth has been working at the restaurant for about three months and she consistently declines invitations to go out with her coworkers. Mostly, she says she's tired and needs her sleep. There is one coworker named Maria whom she's gotten together with for dinner and casual time. Elizabeth likes her and she anticipates a deeper friendship. Even though her work is going well, Elizabeth is beginning to feel that some of her coworkers are becoming distant due to her repeated rejection of their invitations. She doesn't want them to think she's not interested, but she doesn't want to straight-out tell them that she needs to go home and get her sleep because she's bipolar. She also wants to further deepen her connection with Maria.

→ **Tim**

Tim is a high school senior with bipolar disorder who recently moved across the country with his parents as a result of one of their jobs.

He's been developing a friendship with a guy in his new neighborhood who invited him to go skiing for the weekend. Tim was up for that; in fact, he was excited by the prospect of really connecting with someone. So he packed his things, including his medicine. When they were unpacking at the resort, Tim dumped his belongings onto the bed where he would be sleeping and his bottle of lithium fell to the floor. When his friend bent down to pick up the bottle, he quickly glanced at the medicine and said, "Hey, what's this for?" Tim was caught off guard and he awkwardly said, "Nothing, just a supplement I take for allergies." The moment passed without any discussion, but later Tim felt uncomfortable about lying. He also wasn't sure what was behind his friend's question. Was it just curiosity, or was there a hint of negative judgment? He didn't know whether to return to the issue with his friend or just let it be.

→ Monique

Monique is in her last year of college, and she's just returned to campus after Thanksgiving vacation. She's been treated for bipolar since the previous summer, and the first part of fall semester had been good, but because she received her diagnosis while at home, there are many friends at school whom she hasn't yet talked to about it. When she was home again for the Thanksgiving break, she thought she might be slipping into a depression. Her motivation was low and she really wasn't looking forward to the intense academic work that she knew was ahead of her in the next three weeks. During the first couple of days back at school, she missed about half of her classes, and by the end of the week it was clear to her that she was seriously depressed. She could barely get out of bed. Monique had a friend in the college gospel choir who wasn't aware of Monique's condition. She had sent Monique four different text messages in the last two days inquiring where she'd been. On Friday evening there was a knock on Monique's door. She dragged herself out of bed and discovered that her friend from gospel choir had stopped by to check on her.

What to do? Clearly, what all three have in common are relationships where one or more people don't yet know the reality of their bipolar diagnosis. Elizabeth wants to connect with her coworkers but she doesn't want to socialize at the risk of losing sleep. Tim wants to establish new friendships in his new town, but he's afraid of how people will take the news that he's bipolar, especially since he wasn't forthcoming about his medication. Monique's diagnosis was fairly recent and she hasn't shared this information with her full circle of friends. She's hit a wall of depression, and she probably needs some help. A friend is at her door, and Monique struggles with how to "let her in."

Like we said, you will need to decide for yourself how much closeness you want and how much risk you're willing to take. You've probably heard the phrase "no pain, no gain." It's true about relationships, too. Here's the advice we would give Elizabeth, Tim, and Monique.

Elizabeth. Elizabeth is dealing with different levels of desired relationships within the same group. She might consider spending some time just with Maria and explaining to her why she chooses not to go out after the restaurant has closed. In that same conversation she could ask Maria not to tell anyone else about her disorder, at least until she comes to know her coworkers better. With this approach, Elizabeth faces two risks. The first is the uncertainty about how her disclosure will be received. The second is whether or not her privacy will be respected. Her potential gain is a stronger relationship with someone she likes, and if she succeeds with that, then it also might have some beneficial impact on her other coworkers' perception of her.

Tim. Tim is filled with uncertainty. His desire to establish new friendships is strong because of his recent cross-country move. At the same time, he's uncertain about his new friend's reaction to seeing his bottle of lithium. Did the friend know what lithium really is? And if he did, did he think that Tim's response was weird? It probably makes sense for Tim to hold off on saying anything more until he gets to know his friend better. As they hang out together, if Tim finds that his friend seems accepting of people's differences, then there might be a good opening to discuss his bipolar disorder at some future date. Then he could even refer back to the incident of the dropped medicine bottle and say he just hadn't felt ready to discuss his disorder openly. This could repair his friend's sense of being deceived, and it also signals to his friend that Tim values him enough to take the relationship to a deeper level.

Monique. Monique's example isn't just about honesty. It's also about getting help at a time when she really needs it. Sometimes beginning to talk to someone, receiving support, and looking at your immediate strategies for getting help can all be important first steps toward getting back to a healthy place. The worst thing that Monique could do would be to tell her visitor that she was feeling sick and simply return to bed without much interaction.

Roommates

Roommate situations are tricky. Let's face it: sometimes roommates are just people who share living space. Your lifestyles may be quite different. You may not even like one another, but you've somehow wound up living together. On the other hand, sometimes you do become close with roommates or you knew each other well before choosing to live together. But however you all got there, you're sharing living space, and your roommates will know details of your day-to-day patterns that people who live separately from you will not know. So what do you do?

In most circumstances, you'll want those who are living with you to be aware of your disorder in case you become unstable and need help. The risky thing about bipolar mood fluctuations, as we've discussed, is that sometimes they may not be readily apparent to you. That's when it's most important to be living with others who have enough information about you to be in position to recognize when you need help.

Just like Elizabeth and Tim, you may find that others notice your sleep and medication needs or even your saying no to drugs or alcohol. It may be that your bipolar-related needs will require open discussion with those who live with you. It's best to have the discussion before finalizing living arrangements. But even then, you and your roommates may have to revisit the issue in the future.

Granted, sharing your needs with others isn't easy. Typically, during late adolescence and early adulthood you want to feel like you're able to take care of yourself. And most of the time you can. But what about those times when your healthy self-sufficiency doesn't work the way it should? We're talking about those times when you want to reject the notion that you need help because the disorder itself may be preventing you from even knowing what you need. That's precisely when it's important to have roommates who know about your condition and how to help.

So let's assume that you live with several roommates and that you're pretty comfortable with all of them. Now consider the possibility of having a discussion with these roommates and informing them about your disorder. And if that option seems like way too much exposure, consider telling only those roommates with whom you feel sufficiently comfortable. Maybe you'll feel comfortable discussing it with just one of them.

In these discussions you'd share your own understanding of bipolar disorder. You'd let them know that you lead a normal life and that in most respects you're just like most people your age. You'd also let them know that there are times when your bipolar disorder may bring about changes in brain chemistry that can affect your sleep, your feelings, and even your thinking. You'd also tell them that if and when these changes occur, you usually require some adjustment in your medication but that the key is catching the change before things escalate upward or downward. Assuming your roommates are receptive to the information, you might even list the different ways that your bipolar behaviors have shown up in the past, and you'd ask your roommates to come to you and discuss their observations if anything similar were to occur while you're living with them. For the lucky, there's a distinct upside to having your friends know about your illness: they can pick up early warning signs that you've missed or don't yet want to acknowledge.

If you truly want to create a safety net, you might even provide one or more of your roommates with contact information for your parents, your psychiatrist, or others you want notified in the event that you need help. You get to decide whom you want to include in the safety net, person by person. Who do you trust to help you? When it comes to your own health and well-being, you can't really go wrong when you opt for more safety.

Before going further, let's pause and do a brief reality check. Take a moment to ask yourself how uncomfortable you felt when you read those recommendations. Possibly you felt very uncomfortable. You might have thought, "No way would I do that!" Who wants to talk with roommates about something that personal? But let's go back to a well-worn metaphor and consider the possibility that you might have type 1 diabetes. Wouldn't you want to inform roommates that if you ever seemed cognitively fuzzy or, worse, unresponsive, they should immediately call 911? Your situation is not all that different.

If your roommates were to find that you're talking uncharacteristically fast, that you seem to be getting by on little or no sleep, or that you're beginning to say things that simply don't make much sense, wouldn't you want them to try to help you before things escalated further? So let's see...you have the option of sharing something very personal in case you might need help, or you have the option of having those you live with remain uninformed, thus increasing the likelihood that your escalating symptoms could result in a bad outcome. The more prudent choice seems obvious, but prudent doesn't mean easy. And sure, these issues are not the typical focus of roommate interactions, but they're common for someone who's bipolar and who's trying to create some safeguards in his or her living space.

One other caution: If at all possible, choose a living situation that can accommodate your lifestyle needs. You may really like and want to share an apartment with the party animals among your friends, but resist the temptation. Remember the four S's of bipolar stability? You need to ask yourself whether you can maintain them while living with particular roommates.

And what about those times when you're living with someone and you just don't connect at all? Maybe you don't want to tell the person because there's some distance or discomfort that you feel with him or her. If you're living with someone you truly don't get along with, then revealing your bipolar condition may not be wise, as it could add to the dissonance in the relationship. On the other hand, if you just don't connect because you have little in common or you move in very different social circles, here again, it's about risk. What do you risk if you disclose your disorder, and what do you risk if you don't disclose it? The answer will vary from one situation to another. The question, however, remains the same.

Love Interests

Coming out to love interests is a bit like coming out to friends. The difference is the amount of emotional risk involved. After all, a broken heart can have serious consequences. From your late teens up through your twenties, the feelings that come with physical and emotional intimacy are very intense. And when relationships progress toward the point when you're making long-term plans, then the implications of being bipolar are also big. All this is uncharted territory because it's new to you. To help you navigate it, we offer four specific questions for you to consider as you approach issues of sexual and emotional intimacy.

First, in considering your approach to a love interest, you need to ask yourself what you're wanting in your emotional and sexual involvement. Is it just a casual hookup, perhaps casual friends with benefits? If that's the case, then whether or not you discuss your bipolar issues is a toss-up.

Just because you've chosen to become sexually involved with someone doesn't necessarily mean that you want to take the relationship to greater emotional depth. You may see someone two or three times and that's it. In that case, what's to be gained by disclosing your disorder?

On the other hand, if you begin a relationship in a casual manner, but you find that you're gradually developing stronger feelings as things unfold, then clearly the stakes are higher and more self-disclosure is important. So the second important question to consider is, How much openness and honesty do you want in the relationship? If the tables were turned, when would you want to be told about something like bipolar disorder? Once you become clear about the degree of honesty you would expect from the other person, then you can see what you yourself need to say or do in order to meet that same expectation.

Now, let's say a relationship has already begun and has progressed beyond the earliest stages. The third question you need to come to terms with is, At what point is it time to talk about your disorder? An alternate way of considering this is to put the question this way: At what point would it seem like you were deceiving the other person by not disclosing your disorder?

If you went out with someone once and you told him or her about being bipolar when you got together a second time, the person probably wouldn't feel deceived or betrayed because you didn't disclose this the first date. However, if you've been going out with someone for three or four months and have avoided discussing your disorder, then yes, it would make sense that the other person might feel deceived. As a consequence, you might also find that the resulting emotional hurt would potentially undermine much of the trust you had established. You may have been trying to protect the relationship, but that can backfire when it comes to withholding important personal information. Taking the risk of self-disclosure at some point sooner than four months in would be more beneficial than harmful to the relationship.

And then there's the experience of meeting someone, really connecting, going out together a few more times, and finding that your feelings are growing much stronger and faster than expected—what we call falling in love, or at least something close to it. This brings us to our fourth question: How rapidly and intensely are feelings developing in the relationship? You can see that same question also has a bearing on the previous two questions. That is, if the intensity between two people develops quickly, honesty and openness develop quickly as well. The intimacy that would seem normal three months into a relationship can become accelerated to three weeks or even three days, depending upon how rapidly and intensely things are happening. Matters of the heart can and do defy prudence that way. Sometimes you and a lover will simply feel caught up in the intense and euphoric feelings of attraction and mutual infatuation. Still, you need to prepare yourself to have the bipolar discussion.

For your review, here are the four questions you should consider as you approach more intimate relationships:

- What is it you're wanting in your emotional and sexual involvement?

- How much openness and honesty do you desire in the relationship?

- At what point is it time to talk about your disorder? (At what point would it seem like you were deceiving the other person by not disclosing your disorder?)

- How rapidly and intensely are feelings developing in the relationship?

In most of your intimate relationships, the other person's acceptance of your bipolar disorder is critical to the future health and development of whatever kind of relationship is established. If you've told the other person at the right time and the result is that he or she pulls back and decides not to be involved with you, then however painful this may be for you, it's important to recognize that this person probably isn't someone with whom you could establish a viable love relationship. And if you find you're completely uncertain about whether to tell about your bipolar earlier or later, our consistent advice is to choose the earlier time. It's better to find out early on that the other person's own biases make the relationship a nonstarter, rather than having to discover it after you've grown deeply attached.

We fully acknowledge that what we're suggesting may feel difficult to do. But the reality is, this same advice applies to most sensitive issues in relationships. We each have our own personal baggage that we bring to our relationships, and being bipolar is more than just a small carry-on bag. But when you stop and think about it, your disclosure of being bipolar simply means it's important for you to be known and accepted for who you are. Isn't that an important condition for emotional intimacy?

Remember, a broken heart is exactly the kind of stress that can turn things upside down for you. When possible, you need to take measures to minimize the damage. Most people are not going to fall in love young, get married to our first love, and live happily ever after. These days it's more common to do some exploring before settling into a long-term commitment. Your bipolar disorder will present unique challenges to a love relationship, and it will be important to connect with someone who's willing to accept and deal with your disorder as it unfolds.

Parents

Some of you may receive your bipolar diagnosis when you are away from home. Perhaps you've been away at college and have been diagnosed while there. Maybe you've graduated and are now living on your own. Or maybe you haven't attended college and have established your own independent life earlier than most. The question in each of these situations is whether or not you share your bipolar diagnosis with your parents.

The answer should reflect the degree of independence that you've established in relation to your parents. That said, when your parents are an important part of your primary support system, then whether or not you're getting along well with them, it's still a good idea to tell them. If you're receiving treatment and there are medical bills or records of insurance billing being mailed to your home, your parents will find out anyway. It's probably better to have a conversation with them up front, rather than during a tense phone call where they're asking about medical bills for blood tests and psychiatric visits. Additionally, despite your best efforts, you may enter a period of instability in which it becomes necessary to interrupt what you're doing and return home for a period of treatment and recuperation. Here again, your parents' support will be very important, as will their need to be fully informed of what's going on with you.

On the other hand, if you are fully independent and well established in your own life, then you may or may not need their support. Your communication with them should be consistent with the way you would share information about any other important event in your life. Quite simply, would it be potentially helpful for them to know?

You'll also recognize that we've consistently encouraged you to put yourself in the place of others, whether they are friends, roommates, or lovers. Let's do the same with parents. Just imagine their first reaction to hearing about your bipolar disorder. It's likely they will feel frightened by the implications of your diagnosis and uncertain as to what they can do to help. As for other reactions: guilt, helplessness, doubt, denial? Sound familiar? Is it really any surprise that your parents will struggle with this information, just as you did at first?

If you're fortunate, they'll simply feel concern and a strong desire to help. This really is the reaction of most parents. However, it's not uncommon for people to find that their parents' reactions are a mixed bag, with some responses that don't feel supportive. If that's the case with you, you might not feel sure you want to discuss your disorder with your parents. In fact, if things with your parents don't feel solid, then you probably have other aspects of your life besides this one that you don't feel like telling them about. So how do you bridge the great divide?

If at all possible, we recommend you have your discussion with your parents face-to-face. You'll have more time for discussion, as well, and you'll have an opportunity to try working through the more complicated aspects of their reactions. We also recommend that you approach the discussion with careful thought about the information you're about to give them. It would be good to discuss the specific difficulties you've had that led you to seek help. It would also be helpful to write down a list of things that you've learned from the mental health professionals who have established your diagnosis. This would include things such as specific diagnosis and treatment recommendations, recommended medicines, and costs of treatment. If you haven't already done so, it would be useful to gather some good written information about bipolar disorder that you can provide to your parents. And if you feel sure that the conversation won't go well, then an alternative approach is to send the news in an e-mail or a letter and let them know you'll follow up with a phone call or a visit to discuss it in more detail. That way they'll have some time to digest the news you're delivering before you try to engage them in discussion.

Remember, you've probably already had some time to deal with the possibility that you are bipolar. For your parents this is new stuff, just as it once was for you. It may take some time for them to adjust to the fact that their child is bipolar. It may even require several discussions with them before they can hear what you're saying and begin to come to terms with it.

One other thing to consider is whether you want your parents to be able to speak directly with the mental health professionals involved in your treatment. If you're eighteen or older, all your treatment information is confidential unless you specifically permit others to have access to it. If you're comfortable with letting your parents have that access, it may be the easiest way for them to become fully informed of what's going on. Signing a release of information will also make it easier for your parents and your treatment professionals to be in communication if that should become necessary in the future. But before you simply say yes to such a release, it's important for you to be clear that this is your choice rather than your obligation.

And if you're under eighteen, what then? Well, legally parents do have access to your treatment information—which means they also have a right to speak with your treatment professionals, even if you would prefer that they don't. However, in most instances you'll find that mental health professionals will at least inform you of what they intend to share with your parents before they do so. This will give you the chance to share any concerns with your treatment professionals.

If you were twelve years old, or if you were thirty-five, your parents' role in all this would be very clear-cut. But most likely you're somewhere in between—no longer a child, but not yet fully adult. Apart from the realities of bipolar disorder, this isn't an easy time. And while support from friends is helpful, support from family is integral to your stability. Even when relationships with your parents are difficult and complex, they're still the people you turn to when you need help. Once you're more securely established in your own adulthood, your reliance upon your parents will change. Until then, though, it's probably important to keep them in the loop of communication.

Teachers and Professors

So why do high school teachers and college professors even belong in this discussion of coming out? Well, the reality is that sometimes your bipolar disorder will affect your ability to perform academically. When it does, you shouldn't have to accept negative impacts your grades, especially when things may be happening that are beyond your control.

Educational institutions are obligated to make appropriate accommodations for individuals with bona fide disabilities. While you may note that we haven't referred to your "disability" thus far, we offer this for your consideration now, thanks to the Americans with Disabilities Act (ADA). The ADA makes provisions for those with physical and mental disorders to receive necessary accommodations that will allow them to do the same academic work that is expected from all other students. In the case of bipolar disorder, this accommodation could take the form of excused absences from class due to an impaired mental state, extended time for test taking, or even adjustments to testing dates and assignment due dates.

The point is, for those of you currently in school, sometimes it's helpful and fully appropriate to discuss your disorder with guidance counselors, teachers, and professors, especially in the context of the ways in which your bipolar disorder is interfering with your academic work. You're better off if you back up these discussions with a brief written note from your treating physician or mental health professional, confirming your diagnosis and the fact that you may be having difficulties with schoolwork.

If you're in the midst of depression or mood instability, sustaining your work effort through a full semester can feel like running a marathon. Help from an understanding teacher or two can certainly relieve some of the pressure. And if doing so helps you sustain reasonable mental health, then it is a wise choice. If your requests are appropriate and are supported by medical documentation, then most of the time you'll find that teachers and professors will understand your situation and be willing to work with you.

the notion of a helping team

If all your efforts have come together successfully—you've received appropriate treatment, remained consistent with your medications, made healthy lifestyle adjustments, and received appropriate support from others—it's reasonable to hope that things have leveled out for you. That said, it's still important to keep in mind that with bipolar disorder, even when you're doing everything right, sometimes things can go wrong. Then what?

Then you reach out for help. The different people we've been discussing in this chapter, as well as those who are providing your psychiatric and mental health treatment, basically make up your personal helping team. These are the people whose help and support should be easily accessible and mobilized if your own efforts aren't adequate to keep you stabilized.

You'll recall that in chapter 4 we discussed the usefulness of a Healthy Actions List. It will also be useful if you have a readily available list of the people you consider to be the essential members of your helping team. These might include people such as your psychotherapist, your psychiatrist, family members, your significant other, roommates, a guidance counselor or academic dean, a supervisor at work, coworkers, close friends, and anyone else you might rely upon to assist you through a difficult time.

Most of the time you're absolutely clear about who these people are and how to reach them. But if you've slid into a strong depression or if you're in the midst of a hypomanic or manic episode, then you can't assume your normal memory and thought processes will serve you effectively. In order to be prepared for this possibility, create a list with the names and contact information of those who are part of your helping team. Ideally this should be kept with your Healthy Actions List and the Symptom Reminder List that we discussed in chapter 4.

Be mindful that the members of your helping team may change depending on where you are. If you go away to school, your helping team there may be different from the one in your hometown. Similarly, if you choose to study abroad, then your helping team will also change with your new location.

In fact, prior to any travel, study abroad, or international job relocation, it would be prudent to investigate what psychiatric resources you'll have available in your new location. If you're going to be away for an extended period of time, then we strongly recommend that you find a psychiatrist who will manage your medications in your new place. Even in this age of global connectivity, you don't want to be three thousand miles away from help at a time when you truly need it.

Doing everything you can to manage your disorder effectively includes being prepared for those times when your own efforts aren't successful. At those times, having a helping team that can be easily contacted and mobilized may make the difference between a moderate shift in mood and a more acute episode where things unravel for you in destructive ways.

the benefit of support from others with bipolar disorder

When you figure that only about 2 percent of the general population of the United States has bipolar disorder, it's not a far stretch to say that you're not going to find many of your peers struggling with the same issues. If you're lucky, you'll be in a place where you'll have access to a support group for people with bipolar disorder. If you're even luckier, the group will be made of people your age. You're most likely to find this if you're attending a large university that has a well-staffed counseling center or mental health services. You may also find appropriate groups at county mental health centers or other community outpatient and mental health clinics.

Don't be surprised if your thoughts about a support group run something like "So first you're asking me to share information about my disorder with friends, roommates, and love interests, and now you're suggesting I do the same with a group of total strangers?!" Yes, we are.

Imagine how you might feel talking with others who are bipolar and hearing that they've struggled with similar issues. Learning about their experience can help you see that your current struggles are not so unusual. When you talk with others who have much in common with you, it can be surprising how rapidly your sense of aloneness or isolation can diminish. Also, you'll reap the benefit of learning about effective strategies from others who have gone through similar struggles. Yes, you'll have to swallow your pride and talk about some of your vulnerabilities, but that's actually a big part of what allows a support group to be successful. It's also a process that can help you to come to terms with being bipolar.

There's no doubt about it: Having a mental disorder is a humbling experience. It's not something you can simply overcome by the force of your will or handle effectively through fierce independence. It's a condition that causes you to recognize the importance of support you receive through the different relationships in your life. None of us are without vulnerabilities, and when we find others whose struggles are similar to our own, we've found gold.

CHAPTER SIX

managing your independence

Most people in their late teens or early twenties want to start creating their own lives. After years of parental and family guidance, the possibilities are exciting. But the choices you're facing are complex. We learn by trial and error, and while this is important experience that almost everyone goes through, because you have bipolar disorder it's especially important for you to be aware of the risks you face as you proceed toward independence.

being involved but not overcommitted

Sometimes you'll find that your newfound independence is like an all-you-can-eat restaurant when you're hungry and everything looks appetizing. There's nothing wrong with having a full plate when you can easily manage it, but you also don't want take on too much only to find that you've underestimated the effort that your commitments will require—especially when you're also trying to manage your bipolar disorder. Jenny's story is an example of this very difficulty:

→ **Jenny**

Jenny had chosen to attend a well-known private university about five hours away from her hometown. She had maintained a high level of extracurricular activities during high school (soccer team, choir, debate club, senior class president), but she had to cut back on things in March of her senior year after she was hospitalized for a week with her first manic episode. After five months of psychotherapy and effective medication, she was excited to get into the swing of things at the university. She thought her sixteen course credits were going to be quite manageable. After all, getting good grades in high school was easy for her. She also wanted to become involved in a couple of university activities at the start of the semester in order to meet new friends and be in sync with others who were making similar commitments.

Fortunately, the debate team was seeking new members, as was the women's glee club. Without hesitation she grabbed at both opportunities. The glee club practiced two afternoons a week and the debate club met one evening weekly for two and a half hours. She discovered that her biology lab occupied the good part of one afternoon, which only left two days when she wasn't scheduled after 3 p.m. Additionally, she was taking an English Lit course with five lengthy novels assigned for this semester. On top of this, Jenny easily connected with her dormitory suitemates, who rarely were in bed and quiet before 1 a.m.

By early November, she found that she was far behind in her academic work. Feeling stressed and frightened, she called her psychiatrist back home, who adjusted her medication doses and made an appointment for a semester break visit, but overall he didn't seem too concerned in his discussion with her.

Jenny felt there was nothing more to do except to immerse herself in course work with whatever free time she had. She also cut back on a couple of hours' sleep each night in order to come up with the extra time she thought was necessary. This strategy didn't work, either, because now she couldn't think as clearly. The harder she tried to keep up, the more frazzled she felt. Even with her intensified efforts she found herself struggling to barely come up with C's and D's. By the time her parents came to pick her up on the day after her last exam, she was again on the verge of mania. The combination of sustained stress and inadequate sleep had taken its toll. Jenny returned home with her parents and was briefly hospitalized. Once stabilized, she entered a period of moderate depression as she found her self-esteem to be in tatters. The strengths she could so readily rely upon during high school hadn't worked as well for her in college, and she didn't know how to get back to her old self.

Jenny's story is pretty common. At first glance, her choices appear reasonable. She took a typical first semester course load which included one basic science. She joined two clubs, a choice that didn't seem excessive to her, given what she was used to in high school. She strongly desired new friendships and welcomed the opportunities that came along.

Now let's look at a few of Jenny's critical mistakes. First, she went forward as if her capacity for stress and high-intensity work were no different than before she developed bipolar disorder. It's likely that Jenny's own denial was at play here, in her wanting to leave her bipolar disorder behind. She assumed that college would be like an extension of high school. This is a common error. Regardless of your success in high school, college-level academic work can be very demanding. Jenny was also overcommitted in extracurricular activities that would consume two afternoons and one evening of her time every week of the semester.

So what should Jenny have done differently? If we look at her initial set of choices, it would have been prudent for her to first find out how demanding university academic work would be before she made additional commitments. Once she felt successful at managing her academics, she could have gradually taken on new commitments. Without that kind of forethought Jenny was quickly in over her head. Another approach would have been for Jenny to drop a couple of courses. This too would have lessened her stress. But the only adjustment she made was to sleep less—which worked against her.

If Jenny was absolutely set on establishing some extracurricular involvement, she could have looked into clubs that required less time. At the beginning of a full semester there are usually many different organizations seeking new members; it's likely there were other clubs available to her that would have required less overall commitment.

Sometimes the choices available on campus are an abundance of competing possibilities. But you'll find that until you have a clear read on your capacity to meet the demands of your new environment, it's better to take it slow. Give yourself at least a month into your first semester before you sign up for any extra stuff.

alcohol, drugs, and partying

For most people, the freedom of first being on your own is exciting. You're no longer under anyone's direct control and influence. Finally, you get to do, say, think, eat, smoke, or drink whatever you want. Granted, you still may face some limitations based on age, but once you reach twenty-one, not only are you fully adult in the eyes of the law, there are no longer any restrictions on your legal right to purchase or consume alcohol.

With this freedom, it's also common to find that people experiment with drugs or alcohol throughout their late teens and twenties. We'd be remiss if we didn't caution against underage drinking or the use of illicit drugs.

Adolescents and young adults often underestimate the risks, but the consequences of being charged with possession or underage drinking will add much unwanted hassle to your life. On the other hand, we also want to acknowledge that underage drinking and drug use do occur, so it's important that you become clear about the healthy choices you'll need to make, especially if you are bipolar.

In recent years research has focused on the importance of tracking blood alcohol concentration (BAC) in order to ensure that behavior isn't impaired by alcohol consumption (Turner, Perkins, and Bauerle 2008). Essentially, this emphasis sends the message to today's young adult that it's not so much a matter of whether you drink, but of how much you drink, the pace of your drinking, and the relationship of these variables to your body weight. In the absence of other risk factors such as family history of alcohol abuse or the presence of medical conditions incompatible with alcohol use, you might even think there's no harm in allowing yourself a couple of drinks, especially if you do so over a period of several hours. After all, alcohol isn't the same as arsenic—right?

We usually drink expecting to feel differently. Without that expectation, why bother? Water, juice, or soda is much cheaper and easier to get. So what's the problem with wanting to feel more relaxed, calm, or socially at ease? Simple: Sometimes you want to feel more than just a little different. If one drink relaxes you a little, then why not feel relaxed a lot? If one drink takes some of the edge off your social anxiety, then why not get rid of the edge entirely? And here's the big one that weighs against the one or two drink proposition: if one drink has you feeling less inhibited and two even less so, what happens to your ability to put the brakes on after two?

One national survey of college students reported that 40 percent of those surveyed acknowledged having between one and four drinks the last time they socialized (American College Health Association–National College Health Assessment 2009). From that same survey, 38 percent, or almost four out of ten students, reported having five or more drinks in one sitting within the previous two weeks. Quite simply, for young adults, having several drinks in a short period of time is not unusual.

More than a drink or two, especially in a brief period of time, can make you silly, loud, gregarious, flirtatious, argumentative, and more. And if you're already feeling down or blue, alcohol can cause those feelings to intensify. When we add the loosening of inhibitions to the mix, which is so common with alcohol use, you'll find you're potentially setting aside your own good judgment and instead being impulsive in ways that aren't typical for you. Many people view this as fun.

But for those who are bipolar, alcohol can be like arsenic. Maintaining emotional stability is essential in the effort to prevent or minimize depressive, hypomanic, or manic episodes. The experience of letting loose is not your friend, regardless of how attractive it may seem when you're with others who are drinking. Peer pressure can increase the risks. Just imagine sitting with a group of friends who are downing shots while you're sipping on a bottle of orange juice. This is a potentially dangerous situation.

One further caution: Being bipolar actually raises your risk for developing an alcohol-related disorder (Goodwin and Jamison 2007). If you're bipolar, it's likely that you'll occasionally experience different mood states that are uncomfortable for you. At these times, the allure of alcohol as self-medication may be powerful. If you're very anxious or irritable, alcohol may temporarily help you to feel calmer. If you're distressed because you can't slow your thoughts in order to get to sleep, then alcohol may temporarily take you into sleepiness. And if you're hypomanic and enjoying it, then alcohol may simply feel like it enhances your pleasure. In other words, alcohol can become an easy prescription for feeling better. Clearly, this is a vicious cycle where the very choices you make to feel better increase your chances of feeling worse. It's not such a mystery that mixing booze with bipolar disorder is a bad idea.

And what about drugs? Much of the caution that we've conveyed about alcohol also applies fully to drug use. What's different is that drugs such as marijuana, cocaine, amphetamines, ecstasy, and LSD can have a greater impact on your brain and your mental processes than one or two drinks of alcohol. Getting high with friends may seem like a harmless thing to do. But think about it. Do you really know what you're getting? Does it have a label certifying its purity and dose? We expect these kinds of guarantees from pharmaceutical drugs prescribed to us and even those can sometimes cause problems. Why would you take such chances with other drugs that affect your neurochemistry? Your emotional stability is too precious to risk being turned upside down by any kind of street drugs. Your journey requires you to be more cautious.

As for partying, it can be fun. But unless you're in a setting where abstinence is a shared norm, partying during the late teens and twenties often involves the presence of alcohol and, possibly, drugs. The university Greek scene typically revolves around drinking and partying. And if you're not in college, it's still true that partying is usually associated with alcohol, drugs, or both.

It's important that you understand we're not coming to this discussion from a moralistic perspective, judging drug- or alcohol-related behavior to be bad or sinful. This isn't our version of *Reefer Madness*. Instead, it's our version of *Living Well with Bipolar Disorder*. We've maintained the position throughout this book that life with bipolar disorder is a different life. This is true, especially when it comes to alcohol, drugs, and partying.

Science shows us that an older brain handles alcohol better (Swartzwelder 2007). If you're both fortunate and successful in managing your mental health over the next ten to fifteen years, then you may find that by your mid-thirties, a beer or a glass of wine with friends will carry far less risk of adverse outcome.

Your challenge is to find and create activities in your life that provide fun and pleasure outside the context of drugs and alcohol. You can be assured there are plenty of other people whose value systems are consistent with that. There are also fraternities and sororities where alcohol isn't central to their activities; their mission has more to do with community service and scholarship. And more generally speaking, whether you're in college or simply out on your own trying to make a decent living, there are plenty of weekend activities that occur away from the bar scene. They may not be so easy to find, but they're out there, and so are the people who value them. If you're attending a college or university, there are typically detailed calendars of university-sponsored events available online. If you aren't in the college scene, similar online information is available for specific geographic regions. Meetups.com is one example of an online organization that brings together people with mutual interests within communities all over the country. Organizations such as this provide opportunities to explore pathways free from drugs and alcohol. Explorations in this direction are crucial to maintaining a healthy lifestyle with bipolar disorder. Clearly you want to connect with your peers. Why not connect with those who share your interests and who also make responsible choices?

continuing your psychiatric treatment away from home

A critical part of managing your independence well is ensuring that you get the consistent psychiatric care you need. Assuming you'll be taking one or more medications over an extended period of time, it's important to have ongoing contact with your prescribing physician. If you're moving more than a few hours away from your hometown, then it's important to transfer your psychiatric treatment to someone who is closer to your new location. To help you evaluate your options, we pose three questions, along with some discussion of the different factors that will influence your decisions.

How long have you been seeing your psychiatrist and how effective are your current medications? If you're in an early phase of treatment where different medication approaches are still being explored, you will need to have more frequent contact with your psychiatrist. Being several hours away will interfere with this process. It would be better to have easy access to the psychiatrist who is managing and adjusting your medication.

If you've got a strong connection with your psychiatrist at home, a relationship of several hours' distance may work. This option is even more realistic if you've been stable on your medication for a long while. If you have, then a psychiatric visit once every two or three months may be enough, as long as you have the option of being seen sooner if you need to. It's also important to note that if your stability unexpectedly changes toward depression or elevated mood, long-distance psychiatric treatment will not serve you.

In your new location, how far will you be from your psychiatrist? Even if you've been doing quite well for some time, mood instability can still occur. This is probably one of the most frustrating aspects of being bipolar. It's also why it's important to have those on your helping team readily accessible when needed. If your new location is more than just a few hours away—for instance, if you've moved from California to Michigan, or something equivalent—relying on psychiatric treatment without the possibility of face-to-face contact isn't a good idea.

Is your new location permanent or temporary? If you're in a phase of your life where you're away from home but still consider your hometown to be your home base, and if you're also doing well and your new location isn't far from home, it may be fine to remain with your home-based psychiatrist. The essential piece here is your ability to regularly return home to see your psychiatrist for follow-up visits.

That said, you still need to be mindful that bipolar instability can occur at any time and without much advance warning. So the ideal is to have a psychiatrist connected with your home base who knows you well. Additionally, you should establish contact with a psychiatrist in your new location, just in case you need to see someone quickly. We're not suggesting that you fully transfer your care, but ultimately, having both bases covered is in your best interest.

And finally, when you do move away from home for good, then it makes sense to establish a psychiatric relationship in your new hometown.

Transitioning Your Psychiatric Care

Once you've decided to see a new psychiatrist, how do you go about finding and transitioning your care to a new professional? Usually the first place to start is with the psychiatrist you've been seeing. He or she may have connections in your new location and may be able to directly assist you in transferring care. If you have friends or relatives in the area where you're moving, they might be able to help with a referral.

If you're relocating to an area with one or more large universities, you can also investigate whether there are any university medical schools in the area. If so, there may be a department of psychiatry that can help you find outpatient treatment.

You will also find that many communities have referral services that you can access through online searches. Additionally, regions throughout the United States typically have community and county mental health clinics. County mental health services usually have limited resources, and wait time for initial appointments can be long. Nonetheless, these may be good sources for referrals.

If you're relocating to attend college or university, we'll address this situation in the next section. But even if you aren't enrolling in college, the professional staff at university counseling and mental health services is typically quite familiar with psychiatric resources for young adults. You can call one of these services and let them know that you're bipolar and need a psychiatric referral in their region. Most likely they will give you the names of several psychiatrists who are known by university staff to provide quality treatment to young adults.

Whenever you're moving your care to a new psychiatric provider, continuity of medical information will greatly smooth the transition. If you've already determined where you will be receiving psychiatric treatment at the new place, it will be helpful to sign a release and have your psychiatrist forward copies of your medical records to the new psychiatrist or clinic. You should also know that your medical records are yours and you have a right to receive copies at any time. During late adolescence and young adulthood, when you're likely to move around, we actually recommend that you maintain a notebook of your medical records so that you can bring copies of your records with you as you move on to college, employment, a job relocation, or whatever's next. Any new psychiatrist can then easily review your previous treatment in order to best serve you in your new location.

University Counseling and Mental Health Services

Most universities provide counseling and psychiatrically oriented mental health services to their enrolled students. These service areas are commonly covered in the same department, usually called something like Counseling and Psychological Services. However, at some universities you'll find that counseling and mental health may actually be split into different service units. There may be something like a University Counseling Center and a separate unit such as Student Health or Mental Health Services, where psychiatric treatment is provided. As each university has its own unique arrangement and specific names for its student services, you'll need to investigate ahead of time. In order to simplify our continued discussion, we'll refer to the generic university counseling center as if it were a full-service treatment setting.

The extent of university counseling services can vary largely from one university to the next. Larger universities tend to have more mental health resources available for their students than do smaller schools. However, this is not necessarily a given, and if you're bipolar you'll want to investigate the mental health resources available to students before you make your final choice of a school. We're not suggesting it should be the only criterion, but it should at least be one of several important factors that you take into consideration. You don't want to find yourself attending a college or university in a rural location where psychiatric services are limited and difficult to access.

Let's assume you're planning on attending a university that is new to you. You're either beginning your freshman year, you're transferring to a different school, or you're entering graduate school. We recommend you contact the counseling center either before you arrive on campus or shortly afterward and make an initial appointment—even if you're doing just fine.

Jenny, if you recall, chose to continue her psychiatric care from home. Unfortunately, when she began experiencing difficulty, the assistance from home was too limited to be effective. Now imagine a different scenario for Jenny: Suppose she had contacted her university's counseling center shortly after arriving on campus. She would have initially been assessed, and the counseling center would have obtained a thorough treatment history. Although she wasn't in need of treatment beyond what she was already receiving, she would already have had a case file opened in her name and a therapist assigned to her if she needed help later on.

In early November, when Jenny recognized she was in over her head, she could have called her counseling center therapist and made an appointment to be seen within a couple of days, rather than having to wait until she returned home at the end of the semester. Also, the new therapist would have obtained a release to confer with Jenny's home psychiatrist and discuss her immediate treatment needs. If both felt that Jenny needed immediate psychiatric assessment, the counseling center therapist would have been able to arrange for her to be seen by a university-based psychiatrist or possibly a psychiatrist in the local community who could make necessary medication changes or take whatever additional action might be needed. The bottom line is that Jenny might have been able to maintain her stability if she had received appropriate help early enough in her first semester. Again, being proactive with your university counseling service and having a helping team available and ready to be mobilized if you need help is far preferable to waiting until your situation has gotten out of hand.

One caution: Often university counseling centers are faced with higher student demand for services than they are easily able to provide. Therefore, it's not uncommon that university counseling centers primarily provide short-term counseling with focus upon stabilization and community referral for longer-term help, if needed. Since your bipolar disorder will be an ongoing issue, don't be surprised if professionals at a university counseling center seem to want to refer you into the local community for longer-term treatment. These practices will vary from one center to the next, but if they talk with you about a referral, don't take this as a rejection. It's simply the reality of the limited resources of many counseling centers.

The Benefit of Continued Psychotherapy

In chapters 2 and 3 we discussed the importance of getting into psychotherapy as a means of helping you to initially come to terms with being bipolar. And while we've been emphasizing the importance of ongoing psychiatric care, do also consider continuing psychotherapy beyond your early adjustment to your diagnosis, perhaps in ongoing weekly sessions over several years. This course of therapy would help you gain considerable insight into the recurring patterns of your behavior. Ongoing therapy would also help you establish a secure foundation of life strategies to manage the ups and downs of your bipolar disorder.

On the other hand, if you're not up for ongoing psychotherapy, you might find great benefit in at least having a therapist you can return to from time to time as needed. And if your time away from home is going to extend over several years, as is the case when you're in college, then you'd be well served by developing a psychotherapy relationship at the new place where you're living. Even if you're doing well, it would be fully appropriate to obtain a referral to a psychotherapist who is very experienced in treating bipolar disorder. Meet with him or her several times, and then consider returning to the therapist at least on an intermittent basis, maybe once a month or so. Later, if you experience a period of instability and need to see someone more frequently, you'll have a good foundation with this therapist.

academic parachutes: course drops and full medical withdrawals

College is stressful. Over a sixteen-week semester, the pressure can build and build until the last few weeks, when you can feel like you're in a pressure cooker. If you're on top of things academically and other aspects of your life are good, then there's no reason why you can't manage the pressure. But what if you're in the midst of a depressive funk and you just can't get motivated? Or what if you keep spiking with brief episodes of hypomania and the medication you've been prescribed happens to knock you out until noon? These kinds of challenges can really handicap you when you're also trying to manage intense academic pressure. Sometimes, even if you're doing relatively well, the academic stress can become the proverbial last straw that causes your mood to tip one way or the other.

When you think of Jenny's first-semester struggles, you'll recall that one of the options she should have considered was to drop one or more courses. Many universities have course drop policies, though the specifics of the policies can vary widely from one school to the next. Understandably, you want full credit for each course you take. After all, each course brings you one step closer to graduation. But when the effects of your disorder are interfering with your ability to complete your academic work, sometimes dropping a course is your best option. The alternative, which is to ramp up your efforts and stay with the stress, doesn't necessarily take you toward positive outcomes. Consider what happened to Jenny by the end of her first semester. If you're currently enrolled or thinking about enrolling in college in the foreseeable future, it's important for you to be familiar with your school's course drop policy and to know how to drop a course if you need to.

Even if you've chosen to drop a course or two, your semester may still become derailed as a result of bipolar mood swings. If this occurs, colleges and universities will usually work with you to process a medical withdrawal. Leaving for the semester or possibly longer will give you time to get well. You will need to discuss this option with your academic dean or advisor, and you'll also need appropriate documentation from your mental health professional.

A medical withdrawal doesn't hurt your academic record. Your transcript will not say "withdrawal due to bipolar instability." For most schools, there is simply a notation that says "withdrawal" or "medical withdrawal," regardless of the malady.

The bottom line is it's important to recognize when your work is faltering because of your disorder. When that happens, if you can't make other adjustments to get back on track academically, then you need to lessen your load or even let go of enrollment altogether. Having to drop a course or temporarily withdraw from college doesn't mean you're not suited for university work; it means your bipolar disorder is temporarily getting in the way.

Despite what you may feel sometimes, there's no rush to get to the finish line. If you don't graduate in four years, jobs after college or more education will still be there. It's also important to acknowledge that your education may take longer because of your disorder. That said, you'll almost never hear someone at age thirty-five or forty lamenting that they hadn't graduated a semester or a year earlier! And while a year or two in your teens or early twenties can seem like an eternity, we promise that the adult world awaits you just around the corner. Right now, you probably can't wait to get there. But if your journey takes a little longer because of bipolar disorder, your options for the future will still remain very alive.

CHAPTER SEVEN

looking forward

By now, you've come to see that life with bipolar disorder will probably be a different life. It won't necessarily be a bad one. But being bipolar means you have one large variable that's going to affect many of your choices as your future unfolds.

If you were in your fifties and you received news of a major medical diagnosis, it might turn some things upside down. However, in when you're your fifties, many of the choices that shape your life's direction have already been made. Things such as a career, a love partner, where you've chosen to live, whether or not you've had children will have already become part of the story line of your life.

In your late teens or twenties, you're still very much giving shape to this story line. You're dreaming, searching, striving, working, hoping, and sometimes just trying to see what comes next. But unlike most people, you've got this thing called bipolar that you've got to factor into the mix. The big question for you is, What will become of your life as a result of the disorder?

do you have to let go of your hopes and dreams?

Maybe, maybe not. Think about your hopes and dreams in relation to the four S's in chapter 4 and consider this: Can you realistically be successful in maintaining your mood stability in the life you envision?

→ Rubén

Rubén sits in a psychologist's office and tries to wrap his mind around the fact that he won't be able to continue in his university's ROTC program. The implications for his future are almost more than he can take in all at once. It's truly like his hopes and dreams are crashing.

Rubén is the youngest of three brothers and a first-generation Latino college student who had been hoping to follow in the footsteps of his father, who had enlisted in the marines at eighteen and risen to the rank of sergeant major.

Rubén had been a good student through junior high and high school, with sports often being the strong organizing influence in his world. At age sixteen he had the opportunity to attend an exhibition of Air Force jet pilots; it was then that he knew what he wanted to do. He couldn't imagine anything more exciting and fulfilling than being a fighter pilot. When he subsequently met with a navy recruiter, it appeared that his ticket to that career was available through university ROTC enrollment.

During Rubén's senior year of high school, his fantasy of becoming a top-gun fighter pilot was amplified by experiences where he was flying high with energy and personal confidence. In his mind, there seemed to be no limit to what he might accomplish. And while he loved this intensity, it also sometimes felt like it was too much, like the energy and expansive thinking were too big to easily contain. At these times the rigors of high school football practice were just what the doctor ordered. An afternoon of blocking, running, and tackling helped Rubén to feel like he could come back down to earth. He also sometimes had his older brother buy him a six-pack, which he used to knock down his energy and help him fall asleep.

Since these strategies seemed to work and Rubén didn't want to consider that anything could possibly be wrong, he pretty much dismissed his energetic spikes as just being a passing phase of adolescence. Besides, sometimes the intense energy was exactly what he needed. It fortified his sense of masculinity, and it served him well with family and friends; among them, competitive intensity wasn't a bad thing to have. Rubén also figured that things would level out once he went away to college and settled into the combination of academics and ROTC military structure.

Rubén was admitted to a well-known university that also provided him a full ROTC scholarship. This was exciting. It meant a college education was possible. He would also be able to bring honor and pride to his family through his own military career.

Rubén's first year at school went well and he felt relieved that his struggles with mood and energy seemed to be over. But his sophomore year was much more challenging. Not only had the work been more difficult, but also Rubén had a harder time keeping things on an even keel throughout fall semester. This was confirmed for him at the beginning of spring semester when his ROTC commander met with Rubén and told him that he wanted him to be seen at the university's counseling center. Rubén was also informed that several other officers on faculty had noticed his intense behavior. Rubén was surprised. After all, wasn't this intensity the very essence of what they were looking for in a naval aviator?

In reality, Rubén's intensity wasn't a good sign. Things hadn't leveled out as he had hoped. In fact, there had been a few incidents where the only way that Rubén could gain some control over his energy was to resort to excessive exercise at the gym or marathon-like runs, sometimes well into the early morning hours. Though no one yet knew how much he was struggling, Rubén did know that whatever was going on with him was more serious than just a passing phase. The fact that others were noticing this intensity and that he was being referred for a mental health evaluation also meant that his high-flying hopes and dreams might have to undergo serious revision.

Now a university psychologist was telling Rubén that he might have something called bipolar disorder, which would likely end his military aspirations. If not a fighter pilot, then what? A teacher? An engineer? Something in the computer sciences? Nothing came close. Absolutely nothing. Rubén felt a strong sense of loss, perhaps more profound than he had ever known. Could he accomplish anything? Could he even finish his college degree? As he began to grasp that his military plans were no longer realistic, Rubén had no idea what he was going to put in their place.

Being Realistic

Rubén's dilemma is that his career-related hopes and dreams were incompatible with the realities of being bipolar. Most likely he would receive medicine to control his mood and energy. This too would be incompatible with ROTC requirements. And even if medication were not an issue, could Rubén truly count on the disorder not getting in the way of his functioning within the military? Life in the military, especially for a fighter pilot, is anything but a low-stress lifestyle. Rubén already knew that his excessive energy sometimes impaired his attention and concentration. He couldn't, in good conscience, place himself in a situation where his instability might put other lives at risk. And certainly the military wouldn't allow that either.

Now let's imagine a very different scenario for Rubén in which he wasn't at all inclined to join the military. In this alternative life track, let's assume he has decided on a career in culinary arts and he's obtained a scholarship to attend a three-year culinary school. His goal is to become a restaurant chef with an emphasis on South American cuisine. In the best of all worlds, let's also assume that Rubén's family, even his career military father, is fully supportive of his choices.

Apart from the unanticipated ups and downs of life with bipolar disorder, there's nothing inherently unhealthy or risky about Rubén's career goals. Probably the biggest risk is that becoming a successful chef is a difficult undertaking. The restaurant business is very demanding, often with extended work hours. Additionally, the experience of working in a busy kitchen is far from stress free. But realistically, isn't that the case with most demanding careers? We don't get to be successful and achieve our goals without undergoing some periods of sustained stress. As we said in chapter 4, your success with bipolar disorder has everything to do with managing your stresses, rather than finding work settings that are stress free.

→ Beth

Beth is a fourth-year medical student trying to make decisions about her area of specialization and her residency options. Early during fall semester she found herself in a frenzy, cleaning her apartment, studying for her licensing exam, completing applications for residencies, and doing it all with a boundless energy. More generally, she tended toward mild depression and low energy, so she found her energetic intensity to be surprising, if not a bit alarming. Given that she was no stranger to episodic depression, she had been curious about bipolar disorder during her third-year psychiatry rotation. Now she was poring over her texts trying to soak up as much information as she could about bipolar hypomania. It was frightening when she saw that she very clearly fit the profile, including the fact that she had been troubled by depression for years prior to the emergence of recent symptoms.

Beth called one of her friends who had already begun a psychiatric residency and described what was going on with her. Her friend was quite concerned, and he took the initiative to call and make arrangements for Beth to be seen for an emergency psychiatric evaluation the following day.

That night Beth found that she couldn't get to sleep at all. Her mind was racing and her body felt like it needed to move in all directions at once. By the time of her appointment the following morning, she was frazzled and also anxious about what she might be told.

After taking a careful history and discussing her current symptoms in detail, the psychiatrist informed Beth that she likely had bipolar disorder. The psychiatrist also recommended that she start a low-dose antipsychotic medicine as well as one of the mood stabilizing medications as soon as possible.

In the following days, Beth found herself reeling from the new information. Bipolar disorder was something she had studied. It was something that happened to patients. It wasn't something that would happen to her! Besides, she had been hoping for a fellowship in cardiology after her residency. She knew this was a rigorous and demanding path involving at least five additional years of residency and fellowship training. She thought she had a good shot at being accepted, but could she really undergo the rigors of repeated sleep deprivation without causing additional bipolar instability?

Beth had spent her last eight years preparing for this next stage of her medical training. She was already $70,000 in debt from medical school. Could she manage the stresses of her final years of medical training? Would it be unhealthy for her? Would she be a danger to her patients? Was she facing a situation where she might have to give up medicine altogether?

These were questions that Beth had difficulty answering, partly because the diagnosis she received was so new to her. The stresses she faced were not much less than what Rubén would have faced had he remained in the military. The difference is that the medical profession would be likely to provide more support for Beth. But would she have enough access to that support during the course of an internal medicine residency and cardiology fellowship? Beth might need to consider a residency more accommodating to her need for a healthy sleep schedule. An even more radical shift would be for her to explore options such as obtaining a research fellowship for a year or two before going on to her residency training. Granted, this detour would delay her progression toward patient care. On the other hand, it would allow her more time to get a sense of the effects of this new diagnosis and to determine what lifestyle management strategies will be essential for her mood stability.

Like Beth and Rubén, you need to take an honest look at the reality of your situation. While you may face some limitations, a broad range of career choices are available to you. Your challenge is to look at the requirements of your career objectives and assess whether those requirements will conflict with your need to maintain mood stability. You must also consider what risks you might face in that career if you were to become unstable.

---

questions about your career choices

1. What are the requirements of your career goals? Given some of the unique needs of living with bipolar disorder, are the requirements achievable?

2. Will your career choice allow you to maintain the kind of lifestyle necessary for stable functioning?

3. Within your desired career, what are the risks to yourself and others if you become unstable? Are these risks worth taking?

Getting a Feel for the Course of Your Disorder

For many people, bipolar disorder represents a large unknown. You may have already obtained a lot of information, but assuming you're still in the early phases of living with bipolar disorder, you're probably still uncertain about the long-range course of your disorder. Okay, so maybe you've had one manic episode and have already spent some time in a hospital. Will this be a recurring experience or will your treatment help to stabilize your disorder over an extended period of time? Perhaps you've already gone through a strong depression that came before or after a hypomanic episode. How successful will you be in avoiding serious depression in the future?

It would be nice if we had a crystal ball that allowed us to see the answers to these questions. Unfortunately, all you've got is your present experience and your intention to try to manage the symptoms of your disorder. You won't know how your symptoms will emerge over time or how successful your treatment will be, at least until you have more experience under your belt.

Our advice is to try to not become fatalistic about the limitations imposed by bipolar disorder. At the same time, you shouldn't be overly optimistic about your ability to manage things. You don't yet know what impact your disorder will have upon your life. You'll know a lot more about being bipolar in two or three years' time. If you can, try to give yourself that much time before you start making big decisions that have long-term implications. Understandably, this may be difficult to do, especially at a time in your life when many people are asking about your plans for the future. Remember, it's okay to say, "I don't know; I'm still working on that one." For most of you, there's still a lot that's going to happen. As the philosopher Joseph Campbell said, "We must be willing to get rid of the life we've planned, so as to have the life that is waiting for us" (Osborn 1991, 18). This is especially true about life with bipolar disorder.

taking stock of your strengths

One myth that we want to debunk is that once you're diagnosed with bipolar disorder you'll become a completely different person. You may have times when your mood or your energy causes you to feel different than usual. You may find that your reactions to some medications will alter your experience some. But that person who sits at the center of it all—you—will continue to be very present in your world.

What frequently does take a hit early on is self-esteem, especially if the symptoms of your disorder have landed you in a hospital, caused a disruption of an academic semester, or wreaked some other kind of havoc upon your life. When these types of things occur, the transient identity of "being a mental patient" can easily overshadow the many other enduring aspects of who you are. In fact, the temporary loss of perception of these aspects of yourself can make it that much harder to regain your hold on your positive self-esteem.

One of the exercises that can be helpful for you is to begin to separate out what is *you* from what is symptomatic of your disorder. And the emphasis here needs to be on that which is you in a positive sense.

Let's assume we're talking with Rubén a couple of months following his initial meeting with a psychologist and his subsequent withdrawal from ROTC. He's begun to get over the initial shock of what's occurred, and he's slowly letting in the reality that he's no longer on track to become a fighter pilot. Understandably, Rubén isn't a happy guy. He's recently been dealt a major blow, but in his day-to-day functioning, he's actually doing okay.

Rubén has begun taking medication. He's had numerous discussions with his family. He's met weekly with the same psychologist. He's also been meeting with staff at the university's career center in order to establish a new set of career goals and an accompanying academic major. So within the broader context of school, career, and all that stuff, Rubén is okay and he's getting the help he needs.

Now as we're sitting with Rubén, let's also assume he's in a good mood. He's had some good interactions with friends today and he's recently begun a relationship that he's enthused about. So we say to Rubén, "When you sit back and think about this guy named Rubén, what do you like about him? What are those Rubén-like qualities that you find to be enjoyable?" Rubén ponders for a few moments and then he says, "He is a straight-up kind of guy. He's not going to let you down. He's hardworking. When he commits to something, he really puts in the necessary effort to make sure it happens. He's funny, but in a subtle kind of way. He's also sensitive to others' feelings—he's not your typical macho guy who doesn't know squat about his or others' emotions. I think girls kind of like him for this reason."

Rubén needs to stop right there and write down his observations. They are not just situational adaptations, nor are they personal characteristics that have little merit or consequence. Rubén described keenly his capacity for commitment, his trustworthiness, a sophisticated sense of humor, and an ability to be in touch with his emotions and to empathize with others.

The point is, with the exception of the very intense mood states and temporary thought distortions that can occur during acute episodes, bipolar disorder isn't going to cause Rubén's personality characteristics to permanently go away. Rubén will have these same capacities in four, six, or nine month's time, unless he happens to be hit with a period of strong mood instability.

Let's imagine that instead of our previous conversation, we're talking with Rubén when he happens to be moderately depressed after a hypomanic relapse. He might be more inclined to say something like "I don't know... He seems kind of dumb sometimes. It's like, what's wrong with him that he can't keep control of his life? You know, one minute he's doing fine, and then the next thing you know he's speaking out inappropriately in class. He doesn't seem to get it that he can being annoying to others. It's more like he's a bull in a china shop. Most people see him that way. And especially with women, once they know he's got a psychiatric disorder, they really want to keep their distance."

When you compare those two sets of comments by Rubén, you're seeing the same person through very different lenses. And though the differences seem so extreme, the truth is they're not that uncommon. When your bipolar disorder takes you into strong mood changes, the accuracy of your self-perception can become distorted.

One way to set up a buffer against these distortions is to take stock of your enduring qualities or characteristics, as Rubén did. Consider the following exercise.

reminders of enduring qualities

- When you think of your positive personality characteristics, the ones that have been present for you over time, what are the first five words or descriptive phrases that come to mind?

- If several of your friends were asked what they enjoyed or valued about you, what would be the top five words or descriptive phrases expressed about you?

Just as we advised Rubén, you should take time to actually write down your responses to these questions. This exercise may feel a bit strange, but writing about your strengths will give you something reassuring to refer to when it's hard to generate those positive feelings on your own. These written affirmations, as well as the Healthy Actions List in chapter 4, will help you in your effort to regain balance. Remember, bipolar disorder doesn't cancel out your enduring positive qualities in one fell swoop. It may throw you off a little, yes, but not forever.

picking yourself up after a fall

What do you do if despite all your efforts to remain stable, things still turn upside down? Remember that whatever you're going through is temporary. Keeping this perspective is one of the more important things you can do to get through rough times.

We can endure a lot when we know it's temporary. Conversely, if we don't maintain that perspective, even a day or two can seem like an eternity.

Just think how miserable you feel when you have a really bad cold, the flu, or bent-over-the-john food poisoning. Knowing that it's not something that's going to hang around forever allows you to hunker down and endure a week of feeling awful. If you thought that being sick with a cold was going to be a permanent situation, the very same experience might be unbearable. With bipolar illness, if you're able to make adjustments in your treatment relatively soon after your mood state has tipped in either direction, then it probably won't take long to return to stability. But even if it takes longer than you anticipated, you still won't be stuck in depression or hypomania forever.

So let's say things have unraveled for you. You're likely to find that you have to rely on others for a while, probably someone central to your helping team. A return to dependency during early adulthood isn't an easy experience. Being hospitalized, returning home, living with family, or even relying on close friends doesn't come easy during your late teens or early twenties. On the other hand, making essential decisions about your life isn't a good idea if your thinking and judgment have been affected by a depressed or elevated mood state. So one of the first things you need in order to get back on your feet is to allow yourself to be helped by others. Exactly what form this help will take will be specific to you. It will be defined by your willingness to trust the guidance and direction you've received from those whom you've trusted before your most recent episode of instability.

An important next step will be a reevaluation of your short-term goals. When you look at where you were headed before things went haywire, can you still realistically get there considering what you've just been through? If not, what adjustments do you need to make?

→ Catherine

As Catherine began her senior year of high school, she already knew that she needed a break. The last two years felt pretty irrelevant as she went through the motions of doing what was expected. Yes, she received reasonable grades, was active on the school newspaper, and even did volunteer work through her church. Her mom and dad were pleased, but she was bored and kind of depressed. In early fall she visited several small northeastern colleges with her parents, but she just didn't feel enthused about her next set of options beyond high school. Life in provincial New England felt too sheltered and limited for her to be very excited about moving forward, especially if the college environment wasn't very different from the social and geographic environment where she was raised.

So she made a deal with her parents: she promised that she would complete her applications to college if she could take a year off with delayed acceptance to school. In the summer after high school graduation, she'd backpack through the Northern Rockies with a close friend. And come September, she'd find a job at a ski resort and spend the next seven or eight months getting a taste of life away from home. She assured her family that after that year, she would indeed continue on to her freshman year. She argued that she had a good track record of being responsible and keeping her promises.

Catherine was surprised and elated when her parents agreed to her plan. She suspected they were too conservative and controlling to trust her with that much freedom. But hey, for the moment she had what she wanted, and it definitely made life more tolerable. In fact, the boredom and alienation she had felt for so long now gave way to excitement about her next year. What she didn't see coming was that the excitement would give way to something much less controllable. By Christmas Catherine was hospitalized after her first manic episode.

Back home, Catherine was relieved to return to the routines that made her life feel normal. She also began weekly psychotherapy with a psychologist who had been referred by the psychiatrist who treated her during her hospitalization. By early spring Catherine pretty much felt like she was back to her old self, and she was again ready to pick up with the plans she had in place before her bipolar diagnosis.

But as Catherine discussed these hopes with her psychotherapist, he cautioned that her plans would place her far from any real support system. And while psychotherapy and medication had made a big difference, it was still too early into her experience with the disorder for her to be sure that she'd continue to be stable. At this stage, there was no guarantee that she wouldn't relapse somewhere between her summer trek to the Rockies and her loosely defined plans for the fall. While independence was tempting, trying to manage on her own could be a stressful experience in itself. Did she really want to put herself in a situation where help and support might not be available if she needed them?

Through further discussion, Catherine recognized that her choice might be a risky one. She decided to stay in the Northeast for the summer and find employment at a residential summer camp. And for now, she would simply wait to see how things developed through the summer before becoming too concrete about her next steps.

Catherine remained convinced that she still wanted a year's break. But she was also aware that the arrival of her new bipolar reality might limit her early strivings toward independence. Taking off on her own to get a taste of independence might not be her best choice. By changing her plans, she could still get away from home while staying within reach of her important support system.

Just as with Beth and Rubén, Catherine's bipolar diagnosis brought new and very important considerations to the table. While sitting in the hospital, she probably felt that everything for the next year or two was ruined. Once she recognized that she could still take her year's break after high school, she could recover some enthusiasm about the near future. Her new plan wasn't as exciting as the big sky Rocky Mountains, but it was safer, and it also allowed for more time to adjust to the reality of her disorder.

As this chapter's examples show, in order to live with bipolar disorder you need to become skilled at continually evaluating and adjusting. Having rigid goals won't work for you; that would be like climbing onto a rodeo bull and being determined to ride a straight line across the arena without visiting the dirt floor. As most experienced riders will tell you, it's not going to happen that way. And most people who have lived with bipolar disorder would agree.

Granted, if you're able to keep working toward living with balance, your ride shouldn't be quite as bumpy as that bull ride. But however rough the ride, your challenge will be to keep a positive attitude so that if you do take a fall, you'll be able to get back up, dust yourself off, and figure out what's next.

will you ever get better?

As to whether you'll ever get better, we can't answer that question with certainty, but we can assure you that the question is one of the most common ones people ask when they are first diagnosed with bipolar disorder.

One reason why the answer is elusive is that mental disorders are not caused by any one thing, and they don't affect just one aspect of your neurobiology. Instead, we're faced with enormously complex variables that influence how each person develops bipolar disorder and subsequently experiences the illness. We're talking about things such as emotional and psychological stability before the illness, genetic vulnerability to the illness, personal lifestyles and environmental stresses. And on top of all this, there's the extraordinarily unique way that each person's mind works. Take all these variables and mix them together, and you've got a lot of unpredictability.

Many research studies have tracked the effects of bipolar disorder on different groups of people over very long periods of time. (These are called longitudinal studies.) In the book *Manic-Depressive Illness: Bipolar Disorders and Recurrent Depression* (Goodwin and Jamison 2007), the authors reviewed most of the important longitudinal studies done to date. In summarizing the findings from these studies, they conclude that up to one-third of patients actually get better and show no further signs of the disorder. Another third are treated and can live reasonable and functional lives. And the remaining third experience continued symptoms with a fair degree of social impairment. If that sounds grim, keep in mind that this bottom third didn't have access to recent improvements in treatment.

So the picture is mixed. There is some good news and there are grounds for hope, based on reports that some people truly do get better. The not-so-good news is that many people with bipolar disorder face a lifelong illness.

And if you're among those with more severe, treatment-resistant symptoms, bipolar can wreak havoc on your life. We don't want to scare you unnecessarily, but we do want you to have a realistic picture of bipolar disorder.

It's also important to recognize that achieving a sense of hope and optimism about your future wellness won't happen if you're passive. Your success in staying out of the bottom third is contingent on your sustained effort to manage your lifestyle. Let's explore this a bit further.

With mental disorders, just as with many physical disorders, we each have our own genetic and constitutional vulnerabilities. You might think of these as being like the strength or weakness of a house's foundation when it's first built. Once you're actually living in the house, you may not have much influence on the house's structural stability. You may put a lot of effort into upkeep and maintenance, but that's not going to determine how well the house withstands a storm. Similarly, in spite of their efforts, some people with bipolar disorder still experience recurrent episodes of instability. Bad genetics, screwed-up brain circuitry, or perhaps a very unstable childhood all work against them. The fact is, there's no guarantee that living well will buy you any insurance against the disruptive aspects of bipolar disorder. Yes, that's the bad news.

But it doesn't mean that you just throw living well out the window. Even if your bipolar life is one of extreme emotional unevenness, your efforts to live well will likely serve as a buffer against things getting even more extreme. Your contributions toward managing your disorder will always make a difference; they just won't serve as a guarantee against instability.

So will you get better? Maybe. For many people, getting better probably means getting better for a while as opposed to forever. And if that stability ends because you slip into a depressed mood or you transition into hypomania or beyond, then that too will have limited duration and you'll get better again. Since your experience will likely be one of changing mood states, perhaps the question isn't so much, Will I ever get better?, but What should I be doing to get better now? And the answer to this question involves much of what you've read thus far. The bottom line is that your chances of remaining well are greatly improved when you understand that healthy living, determination, and positive outcomes are closely intertwined.

creating new hopes and dreams

For most of us, if not all, life isn't smooth. Even those who appear to live bountiful, gifted, and secure lives still struggle with the complexities of their individual worlds. When it comes to suffering, there's no objective scale; everything is relative. We all have our own issues to deal with. Yours may be bipolar issues, but that doesn't mean you're facing a broken life without potential for healing and achievement.

Consider this: Your life won't be one of bland and simple emotions; it will be just the opposite. You may find that your thinking is occasionally accelerated with mental associations that are wide-ranging, expansive, and uniquely creative. Conversely, you may find yourself a frequent traveler in the realm of sadness and melancholy. Quite possibly you'll also live with an emotional sensitivity where even your milder feelings are experienced with depth and texture, while the strong ones may be closer to an emotional tempest.

For some, this emotionally infused temperament can give rise to remarkable degrees of creativity. In fact, if you look at the history of artistic expression, you'll find evidence of intense variable mood states among many of the world's great artists. If the emotional landscapes of our world's best writers, painters, musicians, and actors had been flat, uninspiring, and psychologically bland, chances are they would never have joined the ranks of the great.

The point here is that the emotionality associated with being bipolar isn't a recipe for a screwed-up life. It is what it is: sometimes good, sometimes bad, and often complex. But to your surprise, you just may find you'll develop some unanticipated strengths and sensitivities with this disorder, instead of only being frustrated by its limitations.

And as for your hopes and dreams, with the exception of a few unique ones, you still have a lot of room to achieve. Okay, so you probably won't become a high-profile politician, a fighter pilot, an air traffic controller, or a CIA agent. But if you take just a few possibilities out of the mix, you're still left with plenty of options. The only difference is that from time to time your progress may be temporarily derailed or slowed down. As long as you and a few select others are aware of this possibility, then there's no reason why you shouldn't nurture your goals with the belief that nearly all things are possible.

You've surely heard those human-interest stories where someone experiences a life-altering event, and then after a period of adjustment they continue forward with amazing determination and fortitude. They make films, create new software, design homes, invent new technologies, teach, coach, build bridges, raise children, and contribute to society in many other important ways. Why not you? Why not now?

APPENDIX A

Internet resources

medication-related websites

www.nimh.nih.gov

www.pendulum.org

www.mentalhealth.about.com

www.healthyplace.com/communities/bipolar/index.asp

www.helpguide.org/mental/bipolar_disorder_medications.htm

stress management websites

www.wholisticdev.com/

www.innerhealthstudio.com/

www.aboutstressmanagement.com/

www.allaboutdepression.com/relax/

http://helpguide.org/mental/stress_management_relief_coping.htm

www.helpguide.org/mental/stress_relief_meditation_yoga_relaxation.htm

mindfulness websites

www.lahdini.com/mindfulness

www.mindfulness.org.au/indexw.html

www.mcmanweb.com/mindfulness1.html

http://facesconferences.com/index.php?main_page=mindfulness

www.uvm.edu/~chwb/counseling/mindfulness/mindfulnessaudio.html

www.alternativedepressiontherapy.com/mindfulness-meditation-technique.html

APPENDIX B

using the Sleep, Mood, and Energy Chart

The Sleep, Mood, and Energy Chart is designed to help people with bipolar disorder track trends and changes in three of the key variables that can indicate a significant shift toward either a hypomanic/manic or depressed mood phase.

Sleep: How many hours you slept during the preceding night.

Mood: How you have felt emotionally over the course of your day. Normal means what is generally normal for you when you aren't in an elevated or depressed mood state.

Energy: The amount of physical energy that you generally feel over the course of your day. As with mood, normal reflects what is typical for you when your energy isn't elevated or depressed.

Instructions for charting

1. Enter the date range of the week in the top of the chart.

2. Think of your previous night and look for the row that most closely matches the amount of sleep that you had the night before. Place a mark in that row for that day.

3. Preferably around late afternoon or early evening, take a few moments to reflect upon your mood and energy during the course of your day. Even if you've experienced some variability in mood or energy, try to identify an average that reflects your experience of the day, then place a mark in that row for that day.

4. You can place several weeks of charts in a row and staple them together so that you can see a longer progression of your trends. You could even make your own chart on a computer and extend it to cover an entire month or longer.

Sleep, Mood, and Energy Chart

Sleep, Mood and Energy		Dates: _____ through _____						
		M	T	W	Th	F	Sa	S
Hours of Sleep	12+							
	9–11							
	7–8							
	5–6							
	3–4							
	0–2							
Mood	High							
	Mildly ↑							
	Midrange							
	Mildly ↓							
	Depressed							
Energy Level	High							
	Mildly ↑							
	Midrange							
	Mildly ↓							
	Depressed							

references

American College Health Association–National College Health Assessment, Spring 2008 Reference Group Data Report (Abridged) 2009. *Journal of American College Health* 57:477–488.

Boku, S., S. Nakagawa, M. Takahiro, H. Nishikawa, A. Kato, and Y. Kitaichi. 2009. Glucocorticoids and lithium reciprocally regulate the proliferation of adult dentate gyrus-derived neural precursor cells through gsk-3b and b-catenin/TCF Pathway. *Neuropsychopharmacology.* 34:805–815.

Davis, M., E. Robbins, and M. McKay. 2000. *Relaxation and Stress Reduction Workbook, 6th Edition.* Oakland, CA: New Harbinger Publications.

Goodwin, F. K., and R. K. Jamison. 2007. *Manic Depressive Illness: Bipolar Disorders and Recurrent Depression, 2nd Edition.* New York: Oxford University Press.

Nesse, R., and G. Williams. 1994. *Why We Get Sick: The New Science of Darwinian Medicine.* New York: Vintage Books.

Osborn, D. (ed). 1991. *Reflections on the Art of Living: A Joseph Campbell Companion*. New York: HarperCollins.

Swartzwelder, S. H. 2007. Dude: Where's my car? Alcohol, memory, and the brain. Annual Susan Grossman Memorial Lecture, University of Virginia, October 30.

Turner, J., W. Perkins, and J. Bauerle. 2008. Declining negative consequences related to alcohol misuse among students exposed to a social norms marketing intervention on a college campus. *Journal of American College Health* 57:85–93.

Russ Federman, Ph.D., is director of Counseling and Psychological Services at the University of Virginia and clinical assistant professor in the university's Department of Psychiatry and Neurobiological Sciences. He is a licensed psychologist, a diplomate in clinical psychology through the American Board of Professional Psychology, and a member of the editorial board for the Journal of College Counseling.

J. Anderson Thomson, Jr., MD, is a staff psychiatrist at the University of Virginia's Counseling and Psychological Services in the Department of Student Health. He is a clinical assistant professor in the university's Department of Psychiatry and Neurobiological Sciences. He is also a staff psychiatrist at the University of Virginia's Institute of Law, Psychiatry, and Public Policy and at Region 10 Community Services. He maintains a private practice in Charlottesville, VA.